LEADING FROM THE HEART

21 Successful Business Leaders
Share How To Create a Profitable Enterprise
By Putting Your People and Relationships
At The Heart of Your Business

Edited By Joan Scott & Andrew Priestley

Soul Sister
with love
Tabitha

WMP

Leading From The Heart

Edited By Joan Scott and Andrew Priestley

First published in MARCH 2024

WM Publishing

ISBN 978-1-914265-94-5 ebk

ISBN 978-1-914265-95-2 pbk

A CIP catalogue record for this book is available from the British Library.

Contents

Foreword: The Critical Value

Fabienne Guichon-Lindholm

The heart-centered leader – the critical value for leadership of the future.

The definition of leading from the heart is subjective to perception, but when I asked ChatGPT for a definition, it gave me this:

"This phrase often signifies a leadership style or approach emphasizing empathy, compassion, and emotional intelligence. When someone leads from the heart, they prioritize understanding and connecting with others on a personal level, fostering trust and collaboration within a team or organization."

There is no perfect recipe for leading from the heart because leading from the heart is a compilation of many different components that one can use based on the energy of their team member. Each group has a unique way of connecting and producing together. However, we found some fundamentals across the board, which should always be adapted and customized for the unit.

People come in teams with pre-determined experiences, cultures, beliefs, likes, and dislikes. Being a heart-centered leader means discovering how the team functions.

In this book, you will find many interpretations of leading from the heart, and every single one is correct. There's no judgment to be had; as the reader, you will find your way, connect with particular components, and develop your own philosophy of leading from the heart.

As a global learning and development executive and the author of *Unapologetically Bold - How to Regain Self-confidence Using the Transformation Cycle while Climbing the Corporate Ladder* in my opinion, leading from the heart should most likely involve the following.

- Create an inclusive and safe space where everyone collaborates, helps, and understands each other while recognizing biases.
- Having empathy and connection through creating a sphere of trust while discovering each other and being furiously curious but never judging and fostering inclusion and understanding while inviting the team to participate as much as possible.
- Cultivating Self-Confidence by allowing the team to grow, make mistakes, catch each other, reward and celebrate wins while analyzing the pitfalls.
- Find a common purpose and passion to strengthen the bond between the people and the company or business, keeping the big picture in mind.
- Establish a culture of open communication without fear of retaliation and focus on discussing good ideas while setting aside the not-so-good ones.
- By nature, we all crave for growth and knowledge.
  It is essential to offer individuals opportunities, challenges, empowerment, recognition, and value. These key factors encourage personal growth and lead to a better and more productive society.

- Listen to understand, not to respond. Developing a culture of feedforward is crucial for facilitating a productive and collaborative team environment. Actively listening to your team without interruption is vital to understanding their needs and perspectives. By providing constructive feedback in a positive manner, we can mentor and guide the team towards achieving their goals and improving their performance.
- Last but not least, and possibly the most difficult for most leaders, is to show vulnerability.

In the following pages, you will find many concrete examples similar to the above, all shared with passion and heartfelt experiences.

For example, the beauty and wellness industry needs to improve how it guides individuals and companies. When marketing becomes the defining factor of a company or brand, there is often a gap between how it's portrayed and what is happening in reality.

Leading from the heart is not a concept; it is a philosophy, and it should not be defined by product market trends but by the people in the organization via HR.

Joan mentioned, at the beginning of the book, the generation gaps. For the first time, we have four generations sharing the workforce now, and each comes with a set of expectations, perceptions, and experiences, so it is time to listen and adapt to stay viable for the world and create a culture of growth, diversity, inclusion with a win-win situation for both employees and employers.

I want to thank Joan for taking this initiative to bring to light what is obvious and to drive awareness of the people's transformation in sectors that take great care of consumers, but rarely of its people.

About Fabienne Guichon-Lindholm

Fabienne Guichon-Lindholm, a seasoned global learning and development executive with over three decades of experience in coaching and motivating teams and individuals.

Through her business, Fabienne Lindholm Rev Up Your Life helps professionals – particularly women – to become confident leaders who drive positive change and transformation.

Prior to starting her own company, Fabienne led the global education department of a major cosmetic company, where she supported teams and professionals across the globe. With over 30 years of executive management experience in the beauty and wellness industry, she managed spa teams and operations for luxury hotels like the Waldorf Astoria and multi-location spas in the USA.

In the past ten years, she has focused on learning and development, training, and consulting with thousands of individuals.

Fabienne is a published author of UNAPOLOGETICALLY BOLD – How to Regain Self-Confidence Using the Transformation Cycle While Climbing the Corporate Ladder.

http://www.fabiennegl.com/

Welcome To Leading From The Heart

Joan Scott

By 2030 Millennials will outnumber Boomers, and this brings with it a whole new dynamic, which every aspect of society will need to embrace.

Millennial's value and nurture quality relationships, many seek psychological safety. This term is defined by Amy Edmondson (Author of The Fearless Organisation) as a shared belief by individuals in a team that it's OK to take risks, to speak up, share ideas, express concerns, and to admit to mistakes – without the fear of repercussion or negative consequences.

The workplace is continually changing. Leaders need to strategically reshape their business to embrace, align and develop a relational leadership approach. This might worry leaders who have always favoured an autocratic, rigid, top-down style, as they may fear this softer more compassionate approach is seen as weak and won't deliver business success.

A holistic approach to well-being has to be at the forefront of recruitment, so it forms part of the employee value proposition (EVP). A variety of factors can influence individual's lives and their overall health and well-being, with the right approach a business can see increased staff engagement, improved performance levels and reduced staff turnover.

Many clients also want to find out how businesses operate, and how they treat their teams – this can be a deciding factor in whether they engage with the company. It is clear that internal values, processes and culture can significantly influence external actions, which are both absolutely critical for business success. Companies that operate ethically, morally and with compassion, can see greater brand awareness- they attract and retain talent, and are often trusted and highly respected within their sector.

If you're in a business that is focussed on 'premium' and 'relationships' rather than 'budget' and 'product', then you have to seriously consider the way you lead. Anyone running a business where relationships with clients are fundamental (and when aren't they?) has to assess the quality of these relationships, as its business critical. This includes both internal and external clients; staff and customers.

A clear focus of your team being at the very heart of the company, leads to you treating them exceptionally, and as a consequence they treat their clients well. The attitude of staff to their clients, can often be a reflection of the managements approach to their staff, it speaks volumes and can illuminate internal issues of poor leadership and a lack of values. Putting your team first, nurturing them and leading compassionately can be a major factor for business success.

An example is Singapore Airlines (SIA), they were voted the World's Best Airline at the 2023 World Airline Awards, this was the fifth time they have scooped this award. As well as being the 'best', they are also one of the most profitable airlines. Their -people first; profit follows -approach appears to be a very successful strategy for SIA.

Another company who put people at the heart of their company, is the Ritz-Carlton Group. They are a globally renowned hotel chain, known for their impeccable hospitality, luxury accommodations, and commitment to service.

The genuine concern that the staff display for their guests is at the core of The Ritz-Carlton experience. This care extends to imaginative experiences, unforgettable adventures, thoughtful presents, and facilities.

The company's approach is "We are Ladies and Gentlemen, serving Ladies and Gentlemen." Their Ladies and Gentlemen (their team) are the most important resource in their service commitment to their guests. Their Employee Promise indicates, "By applying the principles of trust, honesty, respect, integrity and commitment, we nurture and maximize talent to the benefit of each individual and the company". This approach demonstrates that the company leads from the heart, with compassion, recognising that their team are the most valuable asset they have.

Accor is a world-leading augmented hospitality Group, with more than 300,000 hospitality experts, they ensure people are at the heart of what they do. They create emotion for their guests, and nurture passion for excellent service. Accor proudly state 'Our strength is our people and caring for them runs deep in our DNA'. This commitment infuses their vision and guides them in their commitment to sustainable progress and empowerment. Taking care of others, starts within their organisation: they strive to support and empower teams. They have gone on to launch their *Heartist* programme, a combination of heart and artist, underlining their team work with their heart and their passion, mastering the fine art of welcoming, connecting and serving others.

Although these companies are global players, the concept of leading from the heart, nurturing your team and acting compassionately is an approach that should be used in companies of all sizes, to ensure growth, success and sustainability.

We can learn from those who have embedded this approach and who have seen huge benefits. In a world where we often have recruitment problems, its critical we look after our people well, support them to thrive and grow with the business, and help them become invaluable ambassadors, so in turn they attract and retain clients as well as other team members. This leading from the heart approach, can be the foundation of the psychological safety that many individuals are seeking.

We are so proud to present 21 successful business leaders who have consciously put people and relationships at the very heart of their business, and created successful, growing, sustainable and profitable enterprises.

In *Leading From The Heart* they share personal, candid stories about what they have works, and the values and philosophy that underpins, shapes and informs and drives their success.

Welcome.

Joan Scott (Editor)

Love And Respect

Samantha Sweet

Love and Respect is the perfect place to start when thinking about our Sweet Squared success story in business! I remember clearly back in 2006 listening to my husband and co-founder Samuel, recording the Sweet Squared out-of-office message. Sam is originally from SLC Utah and has a rich, deep, American accent and as I pressed my ear to his office door, I remember hearing the words… 'and for some patented Love & Respect', press… and I walked away from the door smiling, thinking, 'Wow!' – he just nailed – in three words – who we wanted to be at the very start of our S^2 journey!

Why wouldn't one want to be loved and respected by the company they 'choose' to do business with? My university years were spent working at a top tennis resort on Longboat Key Florida and boy did I learn about customer service. When I eventually made my way back to the UK I had a very specific idea of how customers should be looked after.

In the mid 90's, the UK was still very awkward with their 'customer-service etiquette' and whilst I was working in my mum's salon at that time, I wanted to make a difference. Sam says I have a 'voice' I use when I am not happy about how I am being treated as a customer and he refers to it as my 'Hotel Voice'.

People like to hear their name used, they like a smile and they want to be heard not ignored. I still use my 'Hotel Voice' when I need to!

There are many companies that 'sell' nail, hair and beauty products; most are box-shifters, the product is there and they shift it out of their doors. We're different. If a customer 'chooses' to purchase from us (Sweet Squared), we think they should be treated like royalty! They're spending their hard-earned cash with us so as far as we're concerned Love & Respect goes without saying!

Our industry attracts many opportunists who see a quick or fast way to make a buck! Opportunists aren't here for the good of the industry and most of the time, they're here today and gone tomorrow. To be here 18 years later, isn't easy but there's a reason! We do what we do from the heart. We serve the professional with the soul reason of helping to make them seriously great at what they do, through recognized, awesome brands and excellent education.

We are a very intimate industry (a lot of what we do is very intimate), hand holding, waxing, seeing parts of people that only their other halves might see... we deal with many people from all different types of backgrounds and diverse situations. Everyone has a story! Showing empathy and understanding goes a long way! Knowing your stuff and being able to 'Tek-Talk' is imperative! You have to understand what these guys do for a living... fortunately for both Sam and I we both did nails for a living, so we get it on a deeper level! If you're only about the money, you're not truly helping anyone.

I remember listening to an ex-distributor talking to a customer who was clearly having problems with her nail application techniques. The customer had already spent a lot of money on her education but needed extra help. The answer from the distributor was to drop another £60 for two hours one-to-one even though SHE was the original trainer!

We would have handled that situation very differently. The customer would have been invited to spend a few hours with us free-of-charge, so that we could watch her go through the motions to help figure out why she was experiencing problems. That not only helps the customer learn and get better, it shows she is dealing with a company that cares, with educators that care and that we're not all about the money! We're about making our customers good at their craft, which makes them successful and THAT'S what makes us successful long-term. I can't understand how anyone doesn't understand that chain of events? That one person becomes a forever customer and all because we took the time to listen, to find a solution to her problem whilst making it fun, knowledgeable and worthwhile – not about how much cash we could squeeze out of them!!

I've said this a thousand times, but when you do things for the right reasons, to help someone, to show a kindness, whatever it may be, it goes a long way and within our industry this is what works. You either get it or you don't. This approach wouldn't work in other industries and I am sure the 'suits' would think us mad, but it DOES work within hair and beauty!! Doing things from the heart brings good things to you.

Leading from the heart means learning to listen, to guide, to nurture and to be tough. Sometimes we just need to throw ourselves out of our comfort zone to grow and gain confidence! Learning to lead and run a successful company doesn't just happen and many mistakes can be made. We are blessed with having the best mentor to help guide and push us.

Sam and I have been exceptionally lucky in that we have had Jim Nordstrom to guide us. This has been critical to the success of Sweet Squared. Jim is a man of extreme integrity, loyalty, honesty and he's not afraid to kick your butt too when needed. He is our partner and has guided us both in various ways, for 17 years. We have done three acquisitions together, we have made tough decisions together and we have had the most enormous amount of fun together too – because business SHOULD be fun! Why shouldn't it? This idea of no one speaking to each other, terrified if they give an opinion they might be fired, is miserable and doesn't create an environment where your team would go to bat for you. Our team would!

Decisions we make must be well thought through and executed with honesty, integrity and passion. So many people have egos the size of Brazil that it's all about ME. ME. ME. Running a successful company isn't about ME it's about the entire team and getting the best out of them. It's not all about how many awards you have won (and we have won a lot), but who you have nurtured and watched blossom into a great team player. We have people in their thirties that started with us in their teens. Nail pros that worked in the salon, who now hold marketing positions and they're great at what they do!! Being given opportunities is a blessing and we wouldn't be here today without having been given opportunities from others.

Why do some leaders in industry feel like they always have to be the Big I AM? Sam who is CEO of S^2 never acts like that! He always says the 'fish stinks from the head down' and whilst I'm not particularly fond of this expression, it is the absolute truth. We learnt this well when we both worked under a self-important, dishonest person only interested in feathering his own nest and not interested in the team or the customer. It was an awesome learning experience because it taught us exactly who we didn't want to be in business. I distinctly remember a warehouse team member complimenting this person on his tie. His answer… 'this tie is worth more than your monthly salary'… just wow!

I am sure Sam and I get a lot wrong, but we lead by example. As we have grown (we employ over 100 team members), we do accept that it's not always easy.

We LOVE Patrick Lencioni's 'The Five Dysfunctions of a Team' book (Lencioni. P. (2002) (Jossey-Bass Publications) and we give this out to all newbies who need it, to read. It doesn't take long but it helps create a truly cohesive team who are not afraid to speak their minds, trust in each other, commit to each other, be accountable to each other and get results!!

Valuing your team means treating them as we ourselves would like to be treated. We share our wins and losses and find ways to elevate individuals when appropriate. We have a healthy, happy, contented workforce but it's not perfect – it's always a work in progress and Sam and I are always learning. I guess the day we think we know it all… is the day we should stop!

Sweet Squared HQ is a 31,000 sq.ft. space incorporating a 20,000sq.ft. SquareHouse (why have a Warehouse when you can have a SquareHouse), offices, store and education facilities. The office space is open with only four individual offices that house Sam, our COO, a collaboration room and my office. I choose to sit with our CX (customer experience) team because I love listening to them and helping with customer needs when they're unclear on something; being with them means I am in the thick of it. I just asked them how they felt about me sitting with them and they said they loved it because I teach them new things and they love how I handle situations. I have to say there is much laughter too. Work Hard. Play Hard.

I am obsessed with Trustpilot and I make it my responsibility to answer EVERY single TP review personally. If we get anything less than five stars I am all over it. We recently had a three-star review and our customer was right to point out some website issues we hadn't realized existed. We listened to her and we corrected the situation. That customer made us a better company! Not only that, but she also amended her three star rating to five stars because we had listened! What a win-win!

Honesty is the best policy in any event, but it doesn't always do you any favors... because not everyone values honesty!

We did a lot of trade shows prior to 2020 and our stand was extremely popular and very busy. Trade shows however are places where again, opportunists take advantage and you can find nonprofessionals coming to buy professional products. I have literally sent people away from our stand to buy from our competitors... why? Because we care about who uses our products... our pros have great reputations and we don't want people who don't care about their clients or our industry using the top products we offer. If all we cared about was money – we'd take it from anyone.

That's simply not the case. We care deeply about our industry and how we do business shows that in buckets and spades!!

Those of us that have been weened into the beauty industry, have a real understanding that we are in an industry like no other. We are a very demonstrative bunch! I don't see anyone giving their bank manager a hug after a meeting but so many nail pros and hair stylists get hugs and kisses after they have provided a service.

Nail pros come in all shapes and sizes and although their job is to perform nail and foot services, they do so much more than that!! They become, therapists, doctors, cooks, schoolteachers, sex therapists – you name it, every working nail artist will have hilarious stories to share. Our pros learn to be good listeners and must learn discretion big time! I remember being in a salon with the wife of a well-known businessman and his lover was sitting in another chair, in the salon at the same time! The wife didn't know, but the nail pros all knew because the 'lover' had filled everyone in! Awkward! Discretion is KEY and can be very uncomfortable at times!!

Beauty professionals are often one-man-bands and as such, it can be lonely for them and it's our job to help them and be there for them. I love how interactive our CX team are with our customers. Most of our team have sat behind the beauty desk and know how to truly help our customers on the other end of the phone. They speak from experience and clients feel like they are talking with a friend!! It makes Sam and me so proud!

A key thing we have always done at Sweet Squared, is we sign off emails to anyone and everyone with 'Love & Respect'. There are those that start working with us that might feel awkward in doing so at first, but that doesn't last for long because it permeates everything we do INCLUDING how we treat each other within the business. Those that 'don't get it' don't last for long.

I think we choose our team wisely too; we believe in people, in their personalities, in their passion and excitement for our industry! THOSE people are worth hiring and are worth their weight in gold. There is also an element of learning to trust your gut. It's never let me down yet.

In a nutshell, we started in our garage with a belief in doing what was right for the industry we both love. We could create our company exactly how we wanted it and with the help of incredible like-minded, good people, we're still here doing what we love and still doing it with Love & Respect.

When you do what you love from your heart, knowing you can make a difference to others, you win in so many ways and I believe in this passionately. Do it from the heart, do it the right way – or don't do it at all!

About Samantha Sweet

Samantha has a 30+ year career within the beauty industry. Her early background consisted of waitressing from the age of 14 and after A 'levels, a 4-year stint in Florida where she worked at a top tennis resort and learnt all things 'customer experience' related.

Once back on UK soil in the early 90's, Samantha went full time into her mum and dad's business which was steeped in the very new beauty sector of 'nail enhancements'. It was in 2006 when Samantha and her husband Samuel created Sweet Squared and in 2007 won their first big brand to represent across the UK and ROI – Creative Nail Design - CND™. Fast forward 17 years and Sweet Squared now boasts 18 'best in show' brands that they deliver with 'Love & Respect' to the UK & ROI market.

Samantha works closely with Education, Customer Experience, Sales, Marketing and PR. She is actively involved in trade shows, Fashion Week and social media to keep closely connected to the Sweet Squared customer.

"Serving the Pro is what we love to do more than anything – to empower our creative guys and girls out there to be more than they ever dreamed."

In September 2017, the Sam's and their S^2 Yorkshire based team, moved into a 30,000sq.ft. bespoke new build and have S^2 satellite locations and teams in Edinburgh and Dublin. Samantha was a nominee of 2017 Yorkshire Forward Ladies Business Awards and winner of BABTAC Services to the Nail Industry Award.

In January of 2018, Sweet Squared acquired the ICON company and became the proud distributors for the Kevin Murphy hair brand bringing the S² team to 130 beautiful members who live to 'Serve the Pro with Love & Respect'!

In 2023, Sweet Squared was awarded the sole distribution rights for EPRES launching March 2023, a hair brand with credible science delivering incredible results and in August 2023 Samuel and Samantha were awarded the top Scratch Stars accolade – Services to the Nail Industry! A huge honour for them both!

samantha@sweetsquared.com

https://www.sweetsquared.com

https://www.facebook.com/samantha.sweet.376

https://www.instagram.com/samanthasweet/

https://www.linkedin.com/in/samantha-sweet-b8aa991b/

Leading From The Heart... Is There Any Other Way?

Joan Scott

'When people go to work,
they shouldn't have to leave their hearts at home'

Betty Bender

'You're the heart of the organisation' was a term that I heard so often that I used to roll my eyes and shudder. Initially I thought it was quite an insincere comment, even patronising. I interpreted it as meaning I was soft and not business focused, not someone who could be a great senior leader, or could achieve outstanding results.

My friends even joked about it, laughing and asking '...are you still the heart of the organisation Scottie?' usually followed by a snigger. When it kept being repeated, I decided to unpick what it meant to me, what was my leadership style? Why did I act a certain way? Was it an effective approach? Did I develop a culture where individuals and teams could thrive and where excellence is delivered? I found that my view of leadership (like many other aspects of life) was that it should be heart-led, heart-felt, and wholehearted. Leading from the heart should come naturally to a leader, and is always fit for purpose in leadership roles.

In hindsight, I should have reflected much earlier. Every organisation needs a strong core, surely being 'the heart' could be really positive? …but something didn't add up. I had a feeling that my approach and philosophy were seen by others as weak, almost 'fluffy', without any real substance, or without the ability to achieve great results, or make a huge positive impact. Whereas my view is, that to lead from your heart, to really care for your clients and staff, pays huge dividends, but it isn't an easy option.

It would be far easier to have a brusque, robotic style, simply going through the motions and operating on autopilot. This type of leader is so task orientated that they don't really care how it's done, as long as the target or goal is reached. I often think leadership and management would be so much easier if you didn't care a jot, weren't people focussed and didn't look after your team. But could you really lead like this, and have a clear conscience? Or keep your staff? Or deliver excellence? Or have a successful and well-respected business?

Leading from the heart involves getting tough things done, but in a human way, in a respectful way, in a diplomatic way, in a kind way, and always in the way that you would like to be treated yourself. Personally, I feel it is an approach that perfectly underpins the psychological safety that individuals are seeking within the workplace, and if research is to be believed, this is particularly important to Millennials.

There are seven aspects to my leadership approach that I'd like to share:

1. Authenticity
2. Connection
3. Compassion
4. Wisdom

5. Excellence

6. Wonder

7. Kindness & Gratitude

1. Authenticity

'Put your heart, mind and soul into even the smallest of acts, this is the secret to success.'

Swami Sivananda

My reflections have led me to believe that to be comfortable with who you are in a leadership role, you must be authentic. This is true for life in general, not just when you're in a leadership role. You can't pretend to be a totally different person in the workplace. Your work role is surely just an extension of who you are, just in a different setting.

You can't put your work outfit on and suddenly become this power-crazed, hard-hitting robot -shouting, thumping the desk and scaring people. To me that is where madness lies, trying to live up to an (outdated) image of a powerful leader, sweeping everything aside in your path. If there's a mismatch between your personal and work life, it must surely play havoc with your desire to lead a balanced life, with good mental wellness. The approach I always take is rooted in following your intuition, listening to your heart as well as your gut and always acting with integrity. I don't think you can go wrong with this approach, in life generally, and especially in work. Don't pretend or be false, be you, but the very best version of you. For me, integrity is closely aligned to authenticity, ensure you have a very strong moral compass, always do the right thing, especially when no one is looking...because *you* are looking, and it surely won't resonate well internally with your sense of self respect, if you operate at a low moral level and subconsciously start to feel guilty or are embarrassed about your actions.

2. Connection

'It's only with the heart that you can see rightly; what is essential is invisible to the eye.'

Antoine de Saint-Exupery

Connection to me is paramount. Whether it be connecting to who you really are, to your team, to your partners, to your client - it's all about establishing a genuine connection. The saying goes that 'people buy from people' – you forge business relationships by being open, warm, trustworthy, loyal and respectful. The same goes for the relationship with your team, they also want a manager or leader to be like this, to treat them well and establish a true, genuine connection.

Communication, to me is also key to having a leadership approach that is fit for purpose. Poor communication can bring down teams and even organisations. Stay close to your team – listen, observe, ask, put yourself in their shoes, to really see the situation from their point of view. Listen to really hear.... don't pretend to listen, so you can then put your side of the issue. Connection and communication are critical when you're developing a relational leadership approach and developing a culture of psychological safety. This allows individuals to feel they can speak up, share ideas and admit to mistakes – without the fear of repercussion.

Communication is really important from a business point of view, but also from a personal perspective. Get to know your team really well, so you know what makes them tick and their motivation, values and goals. Be quick to praise, to recognise and celebrate hard work and good results.

Equally be careful to nip any issues in the bud, so it's dealt with diplomatically and appropriately. I see many leaders take the easy option, sweeping issues under the carpet, which prolongs the poor performance or unacceptable behaviours, which then turns into a larger problem. If you don't address these issues, good staff will then see nothing is done about it, that there are no consequences – they lose heart. In turn, this demotivates the rest of the team and they see the management as weak, and they start to question if it's an organisation where they want to stay. Ultimately Leaders always need to model the behaviours they want to see within their team.

3. Compassion

'People do not care how much you know, until they know how much you care.'

John C Maxwell

I think this is one of the fundamental aspects of being a leader - to care, and I mean to really, genuinely care. If you don't care, then my view is you should step aside for someone who does. To be a successful leader, you must genuinely care about your team, about your clients, about your business partners - about people in general.

You can't fake it; you'll always be found out. It's not easy, it takes a huge amount of effort. You're always keeping an eye on your team, and those across the organisation. It takes more time, and it's hard work, as you must ensure all the targets are met, the goals achieved and that your people feel valued, supported and cared for. It takes great strength of character to balance all these aspects, it would be far easier not to care, be heartless and let issues escalate and staff become unsettled and unmotivated.

Organisations are always looking for new ways to attract and retain talent, often it isn't the money or perks they stay for, it can be one small word – care. People will mainly stay where they feel valued, supported, and cared for. In a world where we are experiencing recruitment problems, a simple approach is to value and nurture the team you have, so they want to stay with you and grow with the business.

4. Wisdom

'To handle yourself, use your head; to handle others, use your heart.'

Eleanor Roosevelt

I believe that leaders who are fit for purpose, for their organisation and their environment, should be wise. Wisdom isn't about being clever, it's much more, it's often explained as a combination of experience, knowledge, and good judgement – all essential for a successful leader. Be sure to gain as much experience as you can and lean into new situations so you can develop and grow. Keep learning, continually read, listen to podcasts, attend courses. Do whatever it takes to be an expert in your field.

Develop your intuition, so you get a feel for situations and people, some feel it in their gut, others in their heart. Use your wisdom to assess how you can develop the culture and expectations of the company. Develop good judgement by continually making well-researched decisions, but also embrace mistakes, as long as you can learn from them.

Many say fail quickly… reflect, move on, and try again. You either win in a situation or you learn, both are positive outcomes. I think you also need to show strength of character; be strong, follow your heart and make a real difference. Address toxic situations or toxic people, so the workplace is a healthy environment for all. Your approach shouldn't be about wanting staff to like you, you're not there to be a soft touch. Some managers are liked simply because they let everyone do what they want and don't intervene. They are ineffective leaders and people pleasers. A good leader should have credibility, they should be admired and respected. They achieve excellent results, whilst caring for their people within a healthy work environment.

5. Excellence

'To be successful, you have to have your heart in your business and your business in your heart.'

Thomas J. Watson

Do you always do your best? Try your hardest? And continually reach for levels of excellence? It's a tall order, but it's a goal that will reap huge rewards. Whatever you do, strive to be the best. It doesn't matter if you're in education, customer service, medicine, law or engineering. Your client/customer/students/patients will all expect you to be the very best in your sector.

You need to share your vision across the organisation, as many won't understand the level of excellence you aspire to. They need to see, hear, feel it - then they'll understand your standards and expectations. You'll need to put your whole heart into achieving excellence, it takes a very clear purpose and a huge passion for the task in hand, so that individuals keep working at ever higher standards and achieve excellence.

Excellence should be evident in all aspects of the business. My mantra when it comes to dealing with any issues is to kill them with kindness. This means using an excellent solution, alongside high levels of customer service and kindness. It can reap great results. Research where excellence is to be found in your sector. Which organisations are already delivering it? What are they doing? Can you do even better?

In a college/academy/university environment not only is it essential to deliver excellent inspirational teaching, learning and assessment, but also how you enhance the course with exciting enrichment. This could be masterclasses, guest speakers, trips, visits, exhibitions, conferences, skill competitions, work placement. In this way you can inspire them, help them to develop amazing skills and also enhance their CV, so they are fully prepared for their chosen sector and go on to have amazing careers.

6. Wonder

'I think it matters when someone has a good heart.'

Elon Musk

I love the word WONDER. A sense of wonder can be described as a combination of intrigue, curiosity, admiration, awe, beauty, questioning... so many facets. When you imbue staff with a sense of curiosity I feel it brings th e magic to life, and to the workplace. We want our team to be intrigued about how to make their products better? How to serve clients better? Do they wonder how other organisations do it differently or better? What other opportunities are there? How do they keep evolving? How to keep improving and being ahead of the game?

They may get a feeling of joy in being adventurous, creative and innovative, as well as improving their performance and the success of the business. My approach is always to look for humour in life, it's something I inherited from my father. He worked very hard, but always had a twinkling smile, with a dry Cumbrian sense of humour, which was appreciated by everyone he met. It's not healthy to be serious all the time, we need to be light-hearted when we can be, and where it's appropriate.

To me, humour is absolutely essential to life, including in the workplace. There is definitely a time and a place, but many situations are enhanced by humour. It lightens the load and raises a smile, especially dry humour.

7. Kindness and gratitude

'A grateful heart is a magnet for miracles.'

My last aspect is so important to a life well-lived. Often, we need to put things in perspective, to realise how very lucky we are. I have a quote on my desk that says, 'the things you take for granted, someone else is praying for'. It stops me in my tracks every time. To know that many of the aspects of our lives that we don't give a second thought to, would be someone else's miracle – sight, hearing, a roof over our head, food, water, education… peace.

I also believe that kindness to people and animals is fundamental to life. If you can be anything, be kind. This is equally as important in the workplace. It doesn't cost anything to be kind, and it feels amazing to both the giver and receiver. The quote comes to mind that you catch more flies with honey than vinegar. So, sweeten up, be kind, care…and smile!

And…please don't ever mistake kindness for weakness. It can be the strongest people who are the kindest. It's so important to recognise, appreciate, value and celebrate your staff, and thank them for a job well done. Often individuals only want people to notice them, to see what they are doing and be appreciated, which is the least we can do as leaders.

I can't let the saying 'a grateful heart is a magnet for miracles 'pass without some reference to the magic that you may need to embrace, the power of positive thinking and how you attract more of what you focus on. I don't want to go all woo woo (…well I probably do!) but sometimes you need to believe in things that maybe aren't tangible or explainable – as Walt Disney said -those who don't believe in magic will never find it. So, I'm going to keep believing, and I'll keep sprinkling my famous pixie dust whenever I need that extra help... it really works!

After a lot of reflection, I'm now proud to be called the heart of an organisation. It certainly isn't for cissies, and it's not a soft option. It takes great strength to balance being people-focused and caring, whilst driving performance to reach targets. It would be much easier not to care, but I couldn't live with myself to lead that way. I couldn't pretend, take the salary, and let the staff down. Instead, leading from the heart is so rewarding.

It provides fantastic results in terms of culture, staff morale, staff retention, high performance and an excellent reputation for the organisation.

If we are to provide psychological safety for our team, to ensure they thrive and work well within their teams across the organisation, to me it's definitely a leading from the heart approach that delivers this culture.

I would always say commit to being the best you can be. In uncertain times and environments, you have got to be agile, to pivot and diversify. Being authentic, connecting, with a focus on excellence and leading from your heart, will serve you well. Rather than one person be labelled as the so-called heart of a company, instead each employee should be the collective 'heart', so everyone beats together for the benefit of the whole.

When you think of it, a body is successful and fit for purpose when it's organs are healthy and strong, its systems connect well, all working in synergy to use resources for energy …it's exactly the same with a company and its leaders. You need to develop a strong core, strong systems all supporting the organisation to perform well.

Always take your heart to work; it's not a weak approach, or a time-consuming option. It's the only way to lead truly and authentically, and it's absolutely critical for business success.

'Wherever you go, go with all your heart.'

Confucius

About Joan Scott

Joan is a Beauty and Spa expert, a skills consultant and an award-winning educationalist. Her last senior leadership role in the further education sector was Assistant Principal at Trafford & Stockport College Group in Manchester, leading strategically on apprenticeships and adult learning. She is a Brand Ambassador for WorldSkills UK, believing passionately about the pursuit of technical excellence and the impact of skill competitions, helping learners to go further, faster. Joan has visited WorldSkills competitions across the UK and in Budapest and Abu Dhabi, and was delighted to win the Times Education Supplement (TES) WorldSkills UK Hero Award.

Joan is CEO and Chair of the Hair and Beauty Industry Authority (HABIA), which is the Government recognised Standard Setting Organisation (SSO). She leads the team at HABIA to develop national standards, apprenticeships, endorse high quality CPD courses and promote education, excellence and professionalism. She also hosts 'Education Forums', keeping educators aware of current challenges and opportunities. Joan is author of *The Official Guide to Spa Therapy* and co-author of *Beauty and the Best* and *Fit for purpose Leadership*.

Twitter *@Joanscott_* *@habia_SSB*

Email *Joan.scott@skillsactive.com*

Instagram *@joanscott__* *@habiauk*

Linkedin *Joan Scott*

From Nurse To Founder: My Unexpected Journey In Leadership

Sally Gordon

I don't profess to be an expert in the theory of *Relational Leadership*, it is only really as I've read a little more about it that I have realised that this is essentially what I've been doing unconsciously since starting my business 16 years ago.

This article therefore is very much about how I have done things and what I have learnt along the way, and is not theory based.

My transition from nurse to business owner happened gradually over time, I suppose, as I grew in confidence. I had absolutely no experience in business and felt it would be impossible for someone like me to be successful at it. I perhaps should mention here that something that I have actively done is to surround myself with people who know more than me. At the beginning this wasn't difficult! What this means in practice is listening to other more experienced business leaders – they have so much to offer – and in most cases really want to share their knowledge and see you be successful. I think that sometimes people feel threatened by this, but, take it from me… don't be. I truly believe that I wouldn't be where I am now if it wasn't for me accepting this generous and valuable help and advice.

The business very much grew organically with no real plan of where I wanted to be in the future. For me, it has always been about the people. These include solicitor clients, colleagues (including both employees and freelancers), suppliers, others working to support the industry and even competitors.

Just to provide a bit of background, 'the industry' in my case is that of Clinical Negligence and Personal Injury Litigation. My company supports solicitors in the preparation of their clients' medical records in relation to their claims. At the heart of what we do is an injured client/patient seeking justice and others working hard to improve patient safety.

When I started out it was just me, but even back then I realised that relationships were vital in building my client base. I know it sounds clichéd, but people really *do* buy people. Many solicitors that became clients back in the early days are people I now call friends. I began to realise that when I looked for suppliers, I only chose to work with people that I liked. Then as my business grew and I started to look for staff, I realised that I was applying the same very simple principle.

'Like' is a rather insipid word, so what do I mean by this? Very broadly, I think this means people who hold the same values as you do.

Trying to decide on the most significant value is very difficult. I guess if I had to choose, I would say that the most important one to me is to always treat others as you would expect to be treated yourself. Put another way, it's about respect and setting a good example. I personally think that it's very difficult for you to go wrong if you do this.

It's imperative to understand that this applies to anyone, whoever they are. Whether they are CEO of a large company, a taxi driver, a senior solicitor, the cleaner, a law firm owner, a waiter, a barrister, a shop worker… it doesn't matter, they all deserve to be shown the same level of respect.

To follow on from this, someone that I have read a lot about and admire greatly is the very successful Julian Richer of Richer Sounds. He says, "I've been running my business for 40 years and the overriding thing I've learned is that it's all about the people. If you treat your people right, then they are going to be happier, give a better service, stay with you, they are not going to steal." Obvious really. His book *The Richer Way: How to Get the Best Out of People* is well worth a read.

Another thing that I've always tried to do is to encourage anyone who works for me, no matter how junior they are, to have a voice and make them feel that they can contribute just as much as the next person. It is stressed to them very early on when joining my company, that there is no such thing as a daft question or silly suggestion.

Some of the best ideas have been born out of this approach. Collaboration is actively encouraged between all staff. Building confidence in this way, leads to empowerment and helps each and every person to feel valued and a vital part of the team. Staff who are made to feel worthwhile are less likely to look elsewhere for work, put simply it drives loyalty. Tied in with this is something that I have personally found very difficult to do, and that is allowing others to do things differently to how you might do them. This sometimes leads to them making mistakes, but often leads to them doing things in such a way that is better than you might have done. Both outcomes, in very different ways, can be difficult to swallow! Remember, helping people to develop in this way, helps to provide the reassurance that demonstrates your trust in them, allows them to flourish and ultimately helps in you letting go.

I've always strived to maintain clear communication within the team. When I talk about communication, it's very much about it being a two-way process. In other words, it's as much about listening as it is about talking. When it is necessary to give directions, they should be clear and consistent.

I guess this is something I learnt to perfect during my nursing career, when effective communication could very much mean the difference between life and death. Although the consequences of getting it wrong in business aren't usually as devastating, I think it's still hugely important to work hard to get this right.

One thing that I've always kept in my mind is that I will only ever ask someone to do a job, if it is something that I'd be happy to do myself, or indeed have done myself. I think this goes back to respect and treating others as you would expect to be treated.

It would be wrong not to talk about those things that I personally have found very challenging. I also think that others who lead by putting their people and relationships first, perhaps face the same challenges? An example of this is when you have a member of the team, who despite training and support are unable to perform the role that you need them to. On a few occasions I have held on to people for longer than I should because I have been unable to let them go. This is usually because I empathise with their personal situation and worry about the effect it will have on them and their family. My advice to anyone who finds themselves in this situation is to be honest with them from the beginning when communicating your expectations, their capabilities, and any concerns you may have so that if you need to let them go it's not as much of a shock to them. This can still be done in a kind and compassionate manner.

The other important thing to do is to think carefully about the impact an ineffectual colleague has on the wider team. For them to see a co-worker, who they often know can't do their job, being paid well like everyone else is very dispiriting. You run a serious risk of other hard-working and committed staff members becoming understandably disgruntled and perhaps even leaving. It is worth bearing in mind that this can have a very negative impact on the business.

Another challenge I have had to overcome, although if I'm

honest I'm still working at, is not taking it personally when a staff member chooses to leave. My head tells me 'Of course, I understand this job is too much to do in part-time hours' and 'Of course, I know this is a great opportunity for you', however my heart is telling me 'What have I/we done to make you want to leave?'. Putting this in writing makes it sounds obvious that these are purely business decisions, however this is something that people who lead from the heart perhaps need to continually remind themselves of.

I truly believe that if you can implement everything I have talked about above, it will lead to a happy and fulfilled team who, as a result, provide a superior service and serve their clients better. Without wanting to appear immodest, I guess the 'proof is in the pudding' (sorry, another cliché!) so what I feel is perhaps important to close with, is to tell you where my business is now.

MRC recently won a prestigious award for Medico-Legal Provider of the Year and have been shortlisted for two more. I know that these wouldn't have happened without our incredible team, and without MRC being a happy and rewarding place to work. We get approached regularly by people wanting to come and work for us, and as a result our staff and freelancer numbers continue to grow. Our solicitor clients remain 'highly satisfied' with the service we provide, commenting particularly on our customer service which they tell us goes above and beyond. I believe that it's therefore no coincidence that we are growing substantially and are on target to have our best year yet.

Richer. J. (2020). The Richer Way: How to Get the Best Out of People. Random House Business

About Sally Gordon

Sally began her career in nursing, way back in 1982. After qualifying as an RGN she went on to specialise in the areas of Coronary Care and Cardiology at Wythenshawe Hospital in South Manchester.

She started to become interested in medico-legal work in 1998 and learnt about the preparation of medical records for litigation. She spent many years building her skills whilst continuing to work as a nurse, and then in 2008 Medical Record Collation (MRC) was established. Sally worked out of her back bedroom at home until 2013, when she outgrew it, and took the leap into a commercial space.

MRC continues to grow and have just completed their third office move into larger premises in Altrincham.

Sally is one of the founding members of PAGE (Pagination Accredited Group of Experts) and is currently Chair. The association was established to promote professional standards and best practice in the preparation of medical records for use in litigation.

https://www.medicalrecordcollation.com/

https://www.linkedin.com/in/sallygordon08/

Leading From The Heart

Kay Pennington

You cannot buy leadership; it is a natural gift. It is a connection, an enormously powerful connection that very few people can be the master of.

Leadership is not a cookie cut set of skills that you can learn solely through a diploma or university degree, and neither can you put a time limit on how long it takes to become a leader. It just happens, it evolves and lives naturally, comfortably, it flows, and it grows in a business-like magic.

True leadership is powerful and is the force behind what really moves and shakes and shapes a business. It is not the investment, not the facility or even sometimes the product.

Leadership is the heartbeat, the spirit to decide success.

When I reflect on my career, I have worked for many different leaders. They come in many different shapes and sizes just like the organisations, from the smallest of family run businesses to high street stores, airline services and multi-million-pound operators in the spa industry. I have seen it all, which relates back to my original comment about why leadership isn't a cookie cutter set of skills.

So, what is the definition of a 'leader'? The dictionary says, 'The action of leading a group of people or organisation'.

I would like to focus on the 'action 'part of the above because in my opinion that is where you find the true nectar in leadership.

Three important questions?

1. What is your action as a leader?
2. What are you delivering as a leader?
3. What is your purpose as a leader?

Thoughts?

1. Is it essential to hire only the best talent and filter out the poor performers?
2. Is it about having a robust and shiny business strategy?
3. Is it about getting popularity and winning awards?
4. Is it about your brand image or even your brand story?

From my experience as a leader, the answer is no, none of the thoughts above which are indeed qualities will completely fulfil or fit the skin as a true leader. You may be gifted with them all but without presence and connection none of the other assets matter.

There is nothing more important than the presence of a leader. This may seem obvious, but you wouldn't believe how many line managers, 'bosses', directors or CEO's I have worked for that haven't been present within their business.

There might be a picture of them on the wall in the staff room to remind colleagues and team what they look like! But a memo or business update in an email or the classic annual newsletter, doesn't quite cut it.

True leadership is about being present and showing connection. Through connection comes energy and communication and through communication comes inspiration, motivation and trust. You can command an army through the power of connection, presence and trust.

Trust in the workplace is critical to not only build higher job satisfaction but to also have lasting effects on retention and performance.

I once read an impressive article in a Harvard business review on employee engagement called The Neuroscience of Trust by Paul J Zak. The article reflects on the science and psychological effects of how building trust in the workplace can increase energy levels by 106% and reduce stress by 74%, compared to low trust companies.

To gain trust, you *must* put your people first; and physically engage. You must show up. Public recognition in the workplace via face-to-face gatherings with your teams to recognise excellence is personal and a staple to drive success and best practice.

I have always called them 'power moments', ideally before you start the working day, but anytime will do if it means capturing a moment to connect with your team. There is nothing more euphoric than having a power moment to pause, to stop, to breathe, to reconsider the purpose, achievements, success and goals. To be thankful of all the participation, commitment and be grateful for each other.

A team gathering *is* a power gathering. You can see it and feel the positive energy in the room. Leaders who often check in and engage with their teams in this way are intensifying their team focus. They are reducing stress and strengthening social connection, which in turn releases neurochemicals such as oxytocin and adrenocorticopen, which has attainable effects on the mental ability to reach goals. A natural feel good and self-belief experience.

As a heart-led leader it has always been my motive to see, read and understand my teams. When I say *teams*, I don't just mean the management, but all the layers involved. Everyone involved in the operation must have a voice and be able to share that voice. Walking the floor alongside your team, getting them to share with you what they are proud of, discussing challenges, current ideas and getting their perspective of how they see the business running is priceless but its free!

Holding a morning brief, having lunch where they have lunch, a walk-and-talk to the canteen or to the local shop... it all adds value. An appreciation wall, a Zoom call to acknowledge greatness, are all the moments that create a wholesome and committed team.

When investing into your facility, its crucial to remember back-of-house as well as front-of-house welfare. Of course, we know just how critical it is to provide well for our guests, but so many times companies neglect the welfare and comfort of their staff and too often, staff areas go untouched and unnoticed for many years. Things like adequate seating to sit and have your lunch. Natural light or outside space for employees to rest in their break. Thousands of pounds are spent to decorate client treatment rooms and public reception areas... but what about the staff area? How does the environment affect your team? When was the last time you asked?

A huge part of my 'action 'as a leader has been to deliver motivational briefing sessions with my team and listen to their needs. On many occasions, I have promised a better staff welfare area and delivered. My purpose has always been to put my team first before any shiny new facility or change of strategy.

During my eight years of success in my group spa operations role, overseeing six spa locations with approximately 800 staff, I am proud to say that we had an average retention rate of 73%.

Of course, this wasn't all my doing it was the structure and relationships that we had in place. Even through the pandemic we held a tight knit line of communication, and I took it upon myself to hold weekly Zoom meetings to engage and be present with the teams through tough and lonely times. We called it *light up lockdown.*

My greatest leadership achievement was being awarded World Spa and Wellness Leader in 2021. The response from my team was electric because they definitely knew it was a team result.

Through my career I have made the best friendships and have built a strong network of men and women that I know, forever, will be by my side, as I will theirs. Self-belief and self-worth and keeping it real has always been my mantra and together we encourage each other to achieve our goals

My Leadership Inspiration

Throughout my childhood up until my late teens I was surrounded by strong women and raised around natural leadership activity. I lived with my Nan and my Auntie for many years.

Alice, my Nan, was a natural leader, an extraordinarily strong and focused woman, and a real character. She had a routine and liked to stick to her routines as they were the key to her success. She made it clear what she liked and what she did not! Alice was very loyal and loving. She was warm and cuddly (especially with me), and she was very generous and kind, but she was also very tough. She would fight tooth and nail for her beliefs, and she was vocal about those beliefs and lived by her means.

Women back then still had the same problems as women have today, mental health, anxiety, stress, relationship breakdowns, addictions, insecurity, and health worries, and there were no social media platforms, Audibles or Facebook tools etc to help. It was all face-to-face. I had the experience of seeing a person light up a room, a person who could create vision and a pathway for others to follow. She created movement, inspiration, motivation, and sense of belonging but most of all purpose and she did through building weekly events for women to meet up at her bowling club, to sit outside in nature, drink tea, eat cake, confide in other women and create a sense of belonging and assurance.

Stepping Away From The Past And Into The Future

How many times do we hear the term 'take the emotion out of it'? How is this possible in leadership? To me it is like trying to brew a cup of tea with no teabag. Emotional intelligence is the ability to perceive, interpret, prove, control, evaluate and use emotions effectively. I have read some articles where it is suggested by experts that emotional intelligence is more effective than IQ?

"While being book-smart might help you pass tests, emotional intelligence prepares you for the real world by being aware of feelings of others as well as your own feelings."

Hannah Owens, LMSW

It is important to remind ourselves that the generation currently running the country – the Boomers – are on the decline. A major shift in leadership will be taking place in the future. According to 'The Future of Work 'article by Zurich (published 1st Feb 2024), Gen Z will account for 27% of our workforce by 2025; and will occupy the majority of key leadership roles by 2030.

It is important – now – for you to consider how your leadership style will foster the strengths of this emerging generation of leaders.

This generation have been named the "first global generation" as throughout their whole lives they have been virtually connected to people across the planet through digital channels.

Gen Z are already actively voicing the values they want to experience in the workplace. Studies clearly show, Gen Zers want employers to show how they support people and their planet. Empowerment and flexibility are likely to be important, building positive relationships through a meaningful career is also likely to be high up on the tick list. Diversity, equality, and inclusion are going to be key topics that also resonate with this generation.

We will see another shift in leadership style and approach, and, to end where I began in my chapter, while there is no cookie-cutter set of skills, however, three words that I am sure will always remain paramount to leadership and underpin success are...

Presence, Connection and Purpose.

Kay Pennington

Kay has always been known for her inspirational and motivational leadership, a positive and dynamic expert in the industry with a wealth of experience across the entire beauty and spa sector. From having her own business at the age of 18, Kay's ambitious drive in her career took to work in some of the UK's most prestigious destination spa's along with flying high on-board Richard Branson's Virgin Atlantic first-class aircraft to deliver treatments as an in-flight beauty therapist to the rich and famous.

A go-getter and influencer in the industry, Kay's knowledge of product houses and beauty brands in the industry is vast and she has supported many salons and spa's in setting up and open doors. Kay has operated and managed six destination spa's across UK and Ireland and lead over 800 staff.

In 2020, she was crowned UK Spa Leader for Professional Beauty and in 2021, she was awarded World Spa and Wellness Leader for her demonstrations in leadership and driving best practice.

kaypennpower@outlook.com

Instagram *@kaypennpower*

LinkedIn *Kay Pennington*

Who Cares Wins... A Passionate Hairdresser's Story

Melissa Timperley

I cried in the salon the other day – full-on tears. It wasn't the first time; and it won't be the last. But before I tell you about the cause, a bit of context will help you to understand why.

Seven years ago, aged 24, I started *Melissa Timperley Salons* with just me, rattling round in a three-storey building converted from a public toilet – seriously. I had persuaded the landlord to take a chance on me, and miraculously he did.

I had a dream to fill that cold empty building with great stylists doing superb work, loving what they do, and with clients who would tell the world about us.

Today we are bursting at the seams, with a happy multi-award-winning team of 16, generating sales of £1m+ a year, making a healthy profit, and a salon full of wonderful clients every day.

A warning before you read further though – you won't find any leadership platitudes here. Leadership is hard (if you care about what you do, and about people, that is). It's a story of a young hairstylist who came into business with a vision to be a superb hairdresser, who abruptly discovered that to succeed she needed to be a passionate 'leader'... not just in name, but in action... every single day.

Other names for it might be 'cheerleader' 'visionary' 'counsellor' 'fixer' 'stress absorber' 'negotiator' 'shield'... you get the idea.

Don't get me wrong, these words are not just about my actions – every member of our team plays their own part; and that's why we've won UK Salon of the Year twice, and UK Team of the Year – we understand it's the first time that the same salon has won both awards in the same year.

If you are happy to consider that we are doing some things right, I wanted to share our approach to leading from the heart in three dimensions – Our Clients – Our Team – Our Inspiration.

Perfecting these elements has been critical to our success. Each supports the other two – and if one is missing, it impacts the others. For example, if our team are happy and inspired, that impacts the client experience, and the client experience impacts our salon success… clients come back, and talk about us to their friends and on their socials. Conversely, if a team member is feeling 'down' for whatever reason, it affects their energy, creativity, and inspiration, and that has a knock-on effect on the client experience. That's why, as a team, we see ourselves 'leaders' in our own right; supporting each other on the days when we are not at our best.

I share these practical things in the hope that some will resonate, and you may want to adopt, or adapt, them for your own purpose. They've worked for us, so maybe they will for you too.

So, what have we done? Let's look through the lens of the Client experience first.

Our Clients

We know that we have the power to positively impact how the client feels about themselves through our relationship with them in the salon.

We want clients to feel fully 'Seen, Heard and Understood' when they are with us in the salon - to feel comfortable and 'at home.' That means treating everyone as an individual, no matter what their circumstances and, of course, delivering excellent service and communication before, during, and after the client's visit.

With the help of business psychologists, we've incorporated Seen, Heard and Understood 'moments' into each stage of our client journey. It's challenged us to be even more empathetic and 'present' for every one of our clients - and it's taken our client service to new highs - one that generates a 72% rebooking rate on the day, has given us more than 470 five-star Google reviews, 70% of which relate specifically to the individual care and attention the client has felt when they have been with us.

We do all the physical things you would expect a good salon to do to deliver excellent client care, and we've won awards for it, but what's been missing for us us delivering against their EMOTIONAL needs – delivering what they DON'T EXPECT - remarkable interactions and acts of kindness that they will tell their friends about, and maybe remember for a lifetime.

We've learned from the psychologists that it's about creating 'psychological safety' for clients; allowing them to feel comfortable to be their 'authentic self' when they are with us - and we've trained each member of the team to create that through analysis of our own personality type and thinking patterns - everyone is different. We understand each other much better now, through focusing on team dynamics and where each of our strengths lie.

Here's a few tangible examples of how we want clients to feel, based on the Maya Angelou quote: "People will forget what you said, forget what you did, but will never forget how you made them feel."[1]

- **EQUAL** - We've introduced gender-neutral pricing
- **INCLUDED** - We've got state of the art disabled facilities
- **UNDERSTOOD** - We're Hijab-friendly, understand diversity, neurodiversity, and the need for privacy. We also have 'silent appointments' for those who prefer that approach.
- **CARED FOR** - Complete one to one attention - our stylist stays with the client throughout their visit
- **IMPORTANT** - We have 'no rush' one-hour appointments. No looking at watches or cutting corners to keep to time
- **LISTENED TO** - Our 3C's Consultation - 15 minutes to discuss Cut, Colour and Condition with the client before we start our work. It's the foundation of our client service.

Our Team

We are a young team, with everyone trying to make their own way in the world, not just in the work environment, but in life, with all its ups and downs.

All our team members have 'employed' status with us – and that gives us real cohesiveness and a shared vision of what we are aiming for as a team. We have a culture that aims to support everyone to be their best, in line with our values.

Shared vision and culture aren't always a 'given' in hairdressing, where the trend is strongly moving to hair stylists being self-employed and 'doing their own thing' as a sole trader, whilst working in a salon environment or 'shared space' collective.

For us, just like our approach to clients, we want each member of our team, no matter how long they have been with us at Melissa Timperley, to also feel Seen, Heard and Understood – by both management and their colleagues. That's easy to say as a slogan, but what does it mean in 'real life'... in moments of stress and pressure, and where we must adapt to what the day (life) brings?

I've turned a 'spotlight' onto four areas where leadership and mentoring from the heart has been instrumental in creating inspiration, wellbeing, and personal growth so that everyone sees the salon as a place where they can contribute in their own way...ideas and ways to do things better, and get practical and emotional support.

Leadership Spotlight 1 – Help to create their 'vision'

Each stylist is trained in-house in the Melissa Timperley cutting and colour principles, as well as our Client Service Excellence approach. We all have the same rock-solid foundation and consistency.

On top of that, we hold quarterly 'My Future Vision' one to ones with each member of the team, to talk about how they are doing and what support they would like to reach their future vision. The career path with us is clear, and we've used transparent performance criteria to promote four stylists to Senior and two to Executive stylist this year.

Leadership Spotlight 2 – Motivate, and encourage work/ life balance

We see motivation as much more than just incentives and one-off fun activities – it includes getting work/life balance, sense of direction and wellbeing right too!

What we've done:

- **Increased salaries** – to cope with cost of living, and to recognise that we are professionals (more on this as a postscript)
- **Shortened hours** – to have enough rest and time to relax and re-charge
- **Introduced a profit share** in our MT Masterclass precision cutting education initiative
- **Rotas that give everyone 16 Saturdays a year off** – so they can have a weekend! If you currently work 9-5 Monday to Friday, that doesn't sound like much – but if you work in hairdressing it's a big deal!
- **Run wellbeing days and training** – so that we can be at our best. Some examples include everyone having a Wellbeing App of their choice and team events featuring amongst other techniques Laughter Yoga and EFT tapping.
- **Given private health care to those who want it** – it's a comfort to know you are covered as a professional

Now we get onto the Inspire element of our approach…

Our Inspiration

Leadership Spotlight 3 – Inspire them

What we've done.

- Formed our own Art Team to get everyone involved in entering awards
- Reached the finals of the BHA's and won the Afro Hairdresser of the Year

- We led the creatives at London Fashion Week for product company ABC
- Run in-salon team training on hair loss, trichology, bleach, and eco-friendly use of colour
- Paid for Stylists to go on top class training programmes in our industry, including Wella Master Colour Diploma, Fellowship Colour Project, and Project X year-long programmes

Leadership Spotlight 4 – Instil personal pride in what we do

This is the big one. We in our industry deserve the recognition that we are NOT just hairdressers – we are the professionals who build client's confidence in both the good and the bad times and help them to take on the world. We're scientists, artists, counsellors, chemists, time management experts, friends, architects, diplomats, and transformers all rolled into one - a true professional with finely honed skills who needs to 'get it right' every time for every client. I'm immensely proud to call myself a hairdresser, and I want all the professionals in our team to feel the same way about the value they bring to clients.

So why was I crying in the salon, and what's that got to do with 'leadership'?

It could have been because a client (counsellor/friend) had just told me that the chemotherapy her husband had didn't work and there was no hope; it could have been the frustration of dealing with the local authority for the last 12 months and getting a 'no' decision on a salon development (fixer/negotiator), or it could have been after the stress of dealing with an irate client because their stylist had needed to stay home to look after their poorly child and there were no appointments until weeks later (stress absorber/shield).

No, it was because of a review a client shared with us. It's not remarkable in itself, but it captures exactly what we are trying to do – create remarkable, memorable experiences.

You should know that Mia is our youngest stylist…

By far the best salon I've ever been to. I've never met a hairdresser who could do anything with my curly hair before (I'm 45 so have tried a lot!), but Mia worked miracles. Great consultation and advice, fantastic cut and styling. She also kindly wrote down instructions for me for how to style it myself.

Both our daughters have also been transformed and loved their experience.

It takes us an hour each way to get to the salon, but I will never go anywhere else again. Can't recommend highly enough. All the staff are really friendly and approachable too.

Thank you!

Yes, leadership is hard when it comes from the heart, and you care, but when it has an impact, you feel emotionally that it's all worthwhile. It had been a tough day that day, but Mia and I celebrated that review. We have further to go, but we are getting there.

As the saying goes 'No one cares how much you know, until they know how much you care.' And we care – a lot.

Angelou. M. (2004). The Arts Go To School Edited by David Booth and Masayuki Hachiya. Pembroke Publishers, Markham, Ontario.

About Melissa Timperley

Melissa Timperley is a multi award-winning hairdresser who works with international brands on hair shows and photo shoots. She is owner of Melissa Timperley Salons in Manchester, England, which she opened at age 24. Seven years on, she now leads a team of 16 professionals serving more than 200 clients a week, generating annual sales of £1m+.

The salon has won nearly 20 creative, marketing and client service awards, including Best UK Salon (twice) and Best UK Salon Team, as well as Afro Hairdresser of the Year.

In 2023, she launched MTMasterclass, a subscription-based online Precision Cutting App which has attracted members from all around the world. Alongside salon colleagues, Melissa also runs in-person cutting Masterclasses in the UK.

Melissa is recognised as a strong female entrepreneur and influencer, having finalised for three national female entrepreneur awards. She lives in Manchester with her husband, James, and her sausage dog, Gregg.

Melissa Timperley Salons *www.melissa-salons.com*

Email *melissa@melissa-salons.com*

MTMasterclass *www.mt-masterclass.com*

Email *info@mt-masterclass.com* *melissa@melissa-salons.com*

MTMasterclass App *MTMasterclass* (Apple and Google Stores)

Instagram *@melissasalons* *@mt_masterclass*

LinkedIn *Melissa Timperley*

TikTok *mt.masterclass*

Gentle In Manner, Resolute In Deed

Andrea Simpson

My journey into the beauty industry wouldn't be described as conventional, with many twists, turns and life experiences that has moulded me, influenced my life, my career and people I have met along the way.

Back in the summer of 1986, I board a train at Doncaster station as a young eighteen-year-old, to navigate myself through London and onwards to Guildford to start my career in the British Army. I instinctively knew as I gazed out of the window, my life would never be the same again and it hasn't. My life journey has meant I have lived in many countries, most recently I have called home the Middle East and Jamaica, travelled independently around the world, had many experiences from parachuting to driving challenger tanks, being in Ubers crossing swamps in the USA very late at night after a long flight, in the middle of no-where, to pinch me moments of treating Royalty, winning awards and having a very successful business that I love dearly.

As a woman in a very male dominated environment of the Military, when equality really didn't exist, you had to use your strength and voice of character to lead and be heard. Women did not train with the men, as they do now, they had their own regiment, The Women's Royal Army Corps (WRAC) who were attached to male Regiments, with very limited job roles open to them and a constant battle of sexism in the work and social environment.

"Gentle in Manner, Resolute in Deed."

Women's Royal Army Corps Motto

The WRAC motto has been a constant in my mind and heart through life. It describes well, someone who appears polite, kind and composed in their behaviour or mannerisms' but is also determined, decisive, firm in their actions and someone who balances kindness and strength in their demeanour and determination in their actions.

I learnt quickly not to be a push over, despite being what might have been described then as being 'fluffy' in appearance from my petite stature, blonde hair and feminine nature, but used this with determination to stand out and be different, rather than sharpening the edges of myself in the masculine arena that the Army was then. This paid off as I was promoted very quickly after a tour of Falkland Islands in 1987.

The military thrives on good leadership, but you can't be a good leader without a great team, respect and confidence in each other. This for me was another early lesson of being surrounded by the best and how much better things work when people work together.

I will be forever grateful for the lessons my military service taught me and still do reflect on how it moulded me as the strong, independent women I am today. I am not afraid to be different or scared of stepping out of my comfort zone to take up new challenges and dare to dream.

I guess I am a natural nurturer and have always been drawn to a calmer way of working. You would think someone with a military background would be quite direct and even dictatorial in their leading; there are times when that approach is needed, but I have always found encouraging, being approachable, being prepared to share and listening to people brings out the best in those I choose to work with.

I had always wanted to join the military, but I also wanted to be a beauty therapist. Logic told me a career in the Services had to come first. I entered the beauty industry as a more 'mature' student. I knew I had to work harder, stand out and drive myself forward being a late comer into the industry and couldn't be further apart from the male dominated world of the British Army. I didn't think myself as 'driven' back then, but on reflection I can see now that I wanted so much more than being a traditional therapist.

I was so very fortunate to have an inspirational tutor who saw something in me and steered me right from the start, but what I didn't know then was my journey in this incredible industry had already started to be carved out and I was unconsciously doing, what I now know as manifesting (and something I truly believe in).

I first linked the power of visualisation and making energy waves over 25 years ago. The moment? I was on ESPA training as a therapist, the educator came into the spa straight off a flight from India where she had been training. She had such a presence of calm and magnetic positive energy. She inspired me so much with her gift of Ayurvedic inspiration, travel and an intrinsic, holistic way of treating. There and then, I said to myself 'I want that job!'

Years later, I walked into ESPA house for the interview that would play a huge part of my destiny. I had that same feeling I had when I boarded that train in 1986, the opportunity of a lifetime was going to happen. I never looked back. Susan Harmsworth the Founder of ESPA is still the inspiring light in my approach to life, treatments and vision.

For quite some years, I had the most astonishing role as an International Training Manager for ESPA. I was privileged to train the spa teams with brands such as Mandarin Oriental, Ritz Carlton, One & Only and The Peninsula. Working with these brands who were at the very top echelons of luxury, attention to detail and guest experience, I learnt such a lot from not only how they value their guests, making a moment spent with them very special, but how they all valued each other's responsibilities and expertise both front of house and backstage to make this happen, along with their commitment to training their teams with the best so they could lead the way in excellence.

I spent a lot of time training the teams in the beautiful and breath-taking spa environments of these world leaders. All with an air of calm and wellness at the heart of them, which made a perfect learning environment. Many of the therapists I trained, English wasn't always their first language, sometimes translators were needed, and cultural customs had to be respected. I had to be aware of how I spoke, the tone, the speed and the clarity of my voice and body language, making sure, what I wanted them to learn, was easy to understand. When I was training practical elements, I had to be the expert, didn't want to come across as criticising, which can be detrimental to confidence or ruffle feathers, for example adjusting a movement, posture or even speed of treatment, showing and explaining why it needed to be done in a certain way. I was aware from my life and career experience, a gentle, encouraging manner with a softer approach yet with firm direction, always worked. I had a responsibility to ensure that I delivered the highest standards in training and the therapists had to meet the expectations, delivering their treatments without compromise and play their part in the team that extended globally.

Leading up to that pivotal interview, a vast part of my beauty career had been in education. I had been a National Educator for Crystal Clear and I spent many years lecturing in Further

Education (FE), working with young people from the age of 16, at the same time I gained my teaching degree from Derby University and had a salon with staff.

Teaching in FE meant that I needed to be a strong lead, a role model for the beauty industry, setting the bar, but show a softer side to invest in the students a self-confidence and self-belief with a different way of discipline, autonomy and encouragement in the classroom that they had not had in mainstream school.

Not an easy balance, but a great example of switching an approach to take charge of situations. Years later as a Clinic Manager for a national chain of aesthetic clinics, I had a team consisting of consultants, doctors, nurses and practitioners, all experts in their field and much different demographic from the luxury spa environment that I had worked in, more often, than not the spa's had achieved Forbes five star accolades and graced the pages of Conde Nast. I found in the clinical environment I had to transition, more from a softly-softly approach that transcended being in the spa environment to being more defined, direct and firm, but still without losing who I am naturally in a lead role, with a calm and quiet determination.

Today, my team is myself, my clients, the brands I work with, my business mentor and business group, the experts I use for their skills and time I lack and my industry friends and peers. I respect hugely all of them and learn from them every day. I have built a very successful business through hard work, determination and of course with a sprinkle of manifestation.

I have learnt so many lessons along the way to get to this point but what I have found is surrounding myself with the best of the best is infectious and really changes your mindset and self-belief.

I have been fortunate to have been around industry leaders who stood out from the crowd, followed their dream and faced challenges head on learning and thriving from them.

I have always found them to be so very generous with their experiences, cheerleaders to others, share their support and they all have such a positive vibe that empowers everyone around them. They are quite aware they cannot be the best at everything, so surround themselves with expertise and listen to them. I find it inspiring, that they are not afraid to speak about their vulnerabilities and when things haven't worked out, what they gained positively from it. They have given me a wonderful gift and I hope I can share that same gift and light with others one day.

If ever I am asked, or if someone needs some encouragement to take a big step, I say;

'Grasp every opportunity that comes your way, you will always learn from it, surround yourself with positive people who encourage you to grow, have integrity in your heart, age has no boundaries, don't be scared of your dreams, dust things off that don't work – you tried, you can be gentle and yet determined and always, always believe in you!'

About Andrea Simpson

Andrea Simpson is a renowned and celebrated multi award winning Facialist. Andrea has travelled the world as an international educator and as a solopreneur, successfully established herself as a leading figure and visionary in the beauty industry.

With a remarkable career spanning over 25 years, Andrea's expertise has earned her accolades, solidifying her reputation as a successful businesswoman. Her dedication to innovation and excellence has positioned her as a key opinion leader in the realm of skincare, where she continues to inspire and educate others with her insightful knowledge and passion.

Andrea is a mentor who generously shares her insights and experiences, inspiring others to pursue their dreams and excel. Andrea's journey exemplifies resilience, concept and an unwavering commitment to the beauty industry making her a guiding light for aspiring solopreneurs and skincare therapists alike.

www.andreasimpson.co.uk

www.instagram.com/andreasimpson_facialist

Being Heartfelt

Candice Gardner

I take it you want to have a greater impact. Perhaps achieve more in your interactions, your projects, and your results. Perhaps you want to establish a strong team that can deliver on time and exceed targets. Perhaps you just want to know if you can do more or be more as a leader.

Ha! And so, you have bought a (or maybe another) book to discover more about leading from the heart in anticipation of something profound.

I can't promise to be profound in this chapter, but I do hope that sharing my perspective might be thought provoking. Whether you agree or disagree with me, use these ideas to challenge your thinking and your intentions, and in so doing, you may find you move closer towards your leadership goals and ambitions.

My viewpoint and approach may not be for everyone, and I wouldn't expect it to be. We are each individual and shaped by our experiences. I, like you, are the sum of my life experiences and choices.

I had very different ideas about what I wanted to be when I grew up. Becoming a skin therapist was not even on the list. And yet some early circumstances and choices led me to a career that I am passionate about.

I am sure you have heard it said that 'if you love what you do, you will never work a day in your life'. Attributed to Confucius (although the accuracy of this translation may be disputed), this saying has resonance with me.

Loving what you do also infers that you care about what you are doing. It doesn't mean there are not tough days or difficult conversations that need to be had. Life and business are not easy; often things get complicated. However, when you care, a lot becomes possible.

But! You are about to argue that caring about the result is still caring, even if you don't love what you are doing... Right?

And I will suggest that it is not really the same thing. The care I am talking about is heartfelt. And herein lies the crux of my view on the matter: if you really don't care, you will never lead from the heart.

I wonder... What is your perspective on being heartfelt?

According to the Oxford dictionary, *heartfelt* means showing strong feelings that are sincere.

There are theories, opinions and practices that segment people into 'head' versus 'heart' types. I have seen this applied to leaders too. But here is the thing... Are people, or leaders for that matter, necessarily less heartfelt because they take time to process information, are interested in facts, have a direct or straight forward, no-nonsense communication style, or are perceived to be task oriented?

I would challenge the notion that anyone is 'all head' or 'all heart'. Everyone I have ever met is their own unique blend of head and heart. So, to reassure you, whatever your natural blend, you can lead from the heart whilst maintaining business focus. It is simply a matter of defining what that actually means to you. Presumably that is why you bought this book?

I have something of a reputation for being a bit of a tough nut. And I likely will never be described as an 'emotional' type, but equally I am not emotionless. I've always been rather direct, although I do work hard to be diplomatic, fair, and kind in my observations. I will hold you to high standards and I will tell you exactly where we stand. Whether we are talking about life or leading, I will interrogate your facts and opinions but here is why… I care deeply about three things.

Purpose. Integrity. Growth.

If we can align what we do with what we care about then we are already a good chunk of the way to leading from the heart. For me, it means I always seek the higher purpose because I want to make a difference, I will prioritise our integrity, and I will continuously strive to foster self-belief that enables growth.

Values-led leadership has been gathering momentum in the last decade as we seek to find greater meaning in the work we do. Having purpose can genuinely alter how we feel about the value of our work. It gives us focus, direction and a moral compass that steers the decision making. More than anything, it brings clarity to why we are doing what we are doing. That is essential in making sound choices and delivering the best outcomes.

I always ask myself whether what we are doing is right by the individuals, right by the community, right by the business and right by the industry. That is the integrity bit.

Let's face it... we're never going to get everything right, and even when we do get it right it is rarely perfect. We can only do our best given our knowledge, skills, resources, and priorities at that time. There are going to be occasions when the decision or the action isn't the right one, despite our efforts. Or maybe we got part way to the goal or delivered some success, but we know there is more we can achieve. This is our scope for growth.

My experience tells me we are capable of considerably more than we think we are. Whilst I agree that sometimes an individual can feel at the limit of their capacity, and the right thing to do is to take some time to reset or rebalance, I also know that I have seen people in many extremely challenging situations lean in and achieve extraordinary things against all the odds.

What makes us achieve beyond expectation? Is it more resources? More knowledge and skills? More time? Yes, all of these can play a role.

Leaders need to acknowledge what type of support is needed and address the gaps for each individual member of the team. Of course, how we build knowledge and skills, engineer learning opportunities through experiences, alongside framing and reframing priorities, are all integral to the development of ourselves and those we are leading.

Yet more than any of these, and what is usually missing, is belief. If you believe you can, then you will.

Something I have come to understand is that without belief in potential, and belief in the ability to do more or be more, we will not move forward. And whilst we all have the inherent capacity to achieve our ambitions, we have differing levels of resilience and grit, and thus having a support network and some cheerleaders can make all the difference. The leader and the team can be pivotal in someone reaching their potential. When your people grow, your business grows.

To help an individual or a team grow or improve performance leaders can approach this in one of two ways: *incremental shifts* or by *bold leaps.*

We can stimulate incremental growth through practice, repeated experiences or use training. These are valid but have varying levels of success. Most often these options take too long to affect significant change quickly enough since self-awareness and reflection are not particularly strong skills for most, and implementation of learning or feedback is notoriously poor. Things become frustrating, and tax our resilience. People lose interest, and they may become demoralised when progress is not fast enough. We can inadvertently replace the performance issue with a motivation issue.

My preference is to help my team grow by bold leaps.

When we grow in big leaps, we start to really tap into the upper tiers of Maslow's Hierarchy of Needs. A sense of achievement fuels our self-worth leading to greater drive; that means increased performance and results. The impact is fast. I have witnessed team members suddenly become bolder in their ideas and ambitions, start to take initiative, and push themselves forward as they grow in confidence. They gather growth momentum from their developmental leaps forward.

How do we grow by leaps?

To start, we demonstrate and verbalise our own belief in their potential. We provide clarity on 'why' this should be done and who it will benefit. We enable independence. We trust them to get it done. Alongside this we establish a culture of continuous feedback that not only provides specific advice but zones out to identify the wider areas for development. If we focus too narrowly on the task in our feedback we miss the opportunity for wider application of the learning to all tasks, activities or interactions.

Normalise this way of continuously cross-examining the facts, the project, the activities. Avoid vague sweeping statements. Be specific but avoid nitpicking. Nitpickers are obsessed with finding fault because it is not how they would do it. Only you can do you. So ease up and don't make it personal – it is not and should never be.

How you would do it is possibly not even relevant.

We should be interrogating the intention to see if it aligns with the purpose and the priorities. Do we agree this is the best outcome we can get? Be clear on why and how to take a different action or approach.

We need to get comfortable with challenging our thinking, actions and our work in order to deliver our best. Always be fair in the assessment of any task or project, but fearlessly interrogating is how we grow by leaps.

Let's bring this back to being heartfelt.

I care about how I can help my team and those around me grow beyond their expectations. That starts with my belief in them, and little by little we build their own self-belief.

I also care greatly about the work I do. If I am intentional, purposeful, act with integrity, champion growth that sees beyond limitations, then who knows what can be achieved.

Your values and priorities might be different to mine, but I don't doubt that there are things you care deeply about. If you can define what you care about and stay true to that, you will find your way to lead from the heart.

About Candice Gardner

With 30 years' experience in professional skin care and skin care education, Candice Gardner is an active advocate for technical and vocational training and participates widely in standards development and employer steering to advance the Beauty, Aesthetics and Wellbeing sector.

With a 25 year tenure at global skin care brand Dermalogica, Candice is an experienced leader in skin care service and skills-led education programme design and development.

Candice is a Member of Council for the City & Guilds of London Institute and Princess Royal Training Award Alumna. Holding various advisory and committee roles, including for the British Association of Beauty Therapy and Cosmetology (BABTAC) and the British Beauty Council, she was recognised in 2023 with a BABTAC Beyond Award for contribution to industry.

LinkedIn linkedin.com/in/candice-c-gardner

Instagram @candicecgardner

Storytelling Embodies The Journey

Arif Isikgun

Navigating the intricate landscape of leadership, I found that fostering a team's creativity and individuality is pivotal for success. There is always competition and stress on the journey to success. I experienced this early on at the age of 22, in Selfridges, as one of the youngest managers, successfully leading multiple-million-pound businesses. One of the most fundamental components, if not the most important, was the team I had built around me, how I managed them and how I brought out their best, helping to fulfil their true potential. In the dynamic world of beauty retail, leading by example, encouraging feedback, impassioning through unique storytelling, and embracing vulnerability transformed my managerial role into a catalyst for growth. The ability to create compelling narratives and engage customers resulted in ground-breaking achievements.

Perhaps one of the most challenging situations you must overcome in a working environment is managing people who aren't definitively under your jurisdiction. What I mean by this is that you are working in a climate that has teams from multiple brands or multiple sections that you must encourage, support, grow and nurture to achieve their very best, each not reporting directly to you. Reflecting on these experiences, and when I hit barriers, often self-imposed, I had to find resilience within myself as an individual and understand that management isn't dictatorial. Good management is a combination of things, the primary realisation was that managing and leading correctly greatly encompasses the inclusion of education.

Beauty retail is a fast-paced and ruthless setting and due to my age, I was often looked upon with envy or spoken to as naive, having a team of 25 and later up to 60 – often older and some more experienced than myself. Managing a multi-million business is not an easy thing to accomplish, however, I lead with perseverance, good energy and understanding that we all have aspects of vulnerability, wanting to learn, wanting to engage and to be encouraged. I believe this led to a successful transformation of that business growing and smashing retail launch records. I remember in one situation, with the launch of a new mascara, we successfully created a waiting list of over 10,000 people within one store location alone! This was primarily maximising our customer engagement through the art of storytelling.

To create such a powerful narrative, we started to tease customers and grew hype and anticipation through romanticism.

This was successful and impactful not only by me but also by my team and how they were led. I managed by example, never getting someone to do a job that I, myself, didn't know how to do or wouldn't do. I let people be themselves, and I encouraged individuality, asking for feedback and pushback to challenge ideas and the status quo. This method allowed my team to grow with confidence, feeling that their voices were not only heard but understood, fertilising their development as individuals. I always felt, and still do, that allowing a team's creativity and cultivating independence was one of the most important factors in leading from the heart. It plays directly to me as an individual, but also showcases the best in people.

To be successful, I've come to realise the importance of equipping teams with the tools they need. Effective communication, presented in a manner easily absorbed by the audience, is pivotal.

Leadership transcends mere delegation; it involves creating an environment and fostering conversations that inspire active learning and motivate individuals to excel.

Transitioning into corporate settings, I grappled with defining leadership beyond mere authority. Rising through the ranks of the beauty industry I started to understand that my management style came from a place of training, education and storytelling – evoking deep-seated emotions through the art of conversation.

However, understanding my peers and the disciplines of being commercial, I asked myself, if I'm not micro-managing or leading through an authoritarian position as others around me are doing, am I fit to call myself a leader? If my team are off doing their own thing and working in their unique way, do I have control of the situation? It's easy to feel as though you are not doing a good enough job as the business hangs in the balance. To all of those who have these types of thoughts, I would simply say ask yourself two questions.

1. **Are you in communication with your team?**
   Is it streamlined, and do you feel you understand the current environment? Are they working to the best of their ability and communicating to you not only results but challenges?
   Do they feel they can be fully open and transparent with you?

2. **What is the bottom line?**
   Are the team and business as a whole achieving targets?
   Are you confident that you are making progress and maximising sales/results? Are the team efficient in achieving targets?

If these two things are in place, then you can feel confident that you are on the right track.

Inward reflection is one of the most important things to cultivate and develop your sense of emotional intelligence.

Know who you are, and who you want to be, and most importantly, know what you want to create around you.

As I delved deeper into the intricacies of leadership, I uncovered the nuanced dance between fostering individuality and achieving collective success. Within the dynamic realm of beauty retail, where trends evolve swiftly and consumer demands shift unpredictably, my experience as a manager at a young age exposed me to the challenges and triumphs of leading diverse teams.

Whilst working in Harrods, Selfridges, and Liberty of London, I understood retail, sales, and how great service creates moments of magic for customers. This can be true for all industries–if we create experiences, and everyone is unique in their way of creating these, we can create exceptional experiences at an emotional level that deeply connect with all. After all, isn't being connected the most important thing about human nature, and leading through integrity and understanding these moments are what matter? We should aim to not just create these windows within our customer-facing and service environments, but also within our teams. It is crucial to understand that leading with emotional intelligence will inspire the people around us, significantly aiding their potential.

After managing a global retail brand within the UK, I had 37 stores and had a direct report of 60 members of staff. Of course, with all situations, there are always challenges and difficulties that present. However, I helped navigate certain issues and discovered that it is usually simpler to approach discussion and conversation from a position of understanding. It's also fundamentally important to show empathy and be open towards your vulnerabilities to show your innate humanity. Positions that stem from genuine understanding and vulnerability help to leverage conversations and maintain steadfast relationships within peer groups. I honestly felt that no issue couldn't be resolved, regardless of how detrimentally severe some situations appear to be on the outside; they would never be out of the realms of resolution. There is nothing a simple chat, over a nice cup of tea, cannot solve. Usually, the problem lies in the individual, not having the level of confidence, holding on to a feeling, and not having the tools to correctly identify the ability to overcome certain obstacles.

Frequently, the route of all negative effects is primarily due to the lack of education, not only through communication, but can run through a company. As a leader, we have a moral obligation and must ensure we create a comfortable, progressive, and inviting environment to nurture someone's ability. As the great Greek philosopher Plato said, "Good actions give strength to ourselves and inspire good actions in others."

Approaching discussions from a standpoint of understanding and empathy became a guiding principle. Openness about vulnerabilities and the acknowledgement of innate humanity fostered steadfast relationships within all groups. This approach, rooted in genuine understanding, proved instrumental in navigating challenges and maintaining a harmonious work environment.

The realisation of the transformative power of education and storytelling unfolded gradually. Education, in the context of leadership, extended beyond formal training programs. It encompassed the art of delivering information in a manner that resonated with diverse individuals and often underpinned emotionally.

It took me quite some time to fully realise the innate power in all of us, it was a fundamental part of being a leader and leading through integrity.

One of the frustrations that we all have when trying to educate or allow a team member to absorb a certain point of view is that sometimes it's not understood. Often a negative situation can occur, and negative emotions can start to fester.

One of the biggest learning lines encompassing this train of thought; if someone does not understand the information relayed to them and cannot use that information the way we expect them, it is not that individual's fault. This stems from the way the information is being relayed. It's a hard pill to swallow. However, in my experience, there are no bad people just bad education delivery – excitement, passion and the story are fundamental to empowerment.

This was the pivotal moment when I wanted to make a change. A change not only in my business circumstances but also within the industry itself. The culmination of my life vocation and individual acumen led me on my very own journey. I created Ai Beauty Consultancy – a service-led and eponymous brand that is faceted to underpin my connection to how I had innovated storytelling, nurturing ideals that birthed my career and independent point of view.

Today, Ai Beauty Consultancy is a love letter to education empowering brands, retail and people with positive education that has transformed businesses and made a huge impact within my selector. My proven training programmes and education creation have global reach transforming and enhancing brand-to-client relationships, vastly increasing sales and profits.

As leaders, we need to understand the different facets of people, start identifying the key indicators that make them who they are and adapt the way we deliver information, so it is the most digestible.This means understanding your audience and leading from a place of integrity, empathising with their situation, so we can see from their point of view. To be successful, as leaders, we must create emotional connections. Being successful is showcasing this level of emotional intelligence, bringing out the best in people and creating the most genuine and profitable outcome.

Leaders must grasp the multifaceted nature of their teams.

Identifying key indicators that shape individuals and adapting information delivery; to be more digestible is integral to effective leadership. This requires a deep understanding of the audience, leading from a place of integrity, and empathising with their unique situations.

To be successful ask yourself, have you given your teams the tools they need for success? Are you communicating yourself in a digestible manner that is easily absorbed by your audience? Is your storytelling engaging, passionate and provocative? Leading is more than asking people to do, it's about creating an environment and conversations that inspire active learning, ignite passions, and motivate. If your team are passionate then you are 90% on your way to success – skills can be taught but passion is infused. In the words of self-made billionaire Joe Segal, "Passion is the key to motivation, and motivation is key to success." It is this belief that I have held on to in my career and it helped me achieve my goals and successes. This continues to guide my leadership philosophy, emphasising the heart as the compass for success in both past achievements and future endeavours, whilst also helping build my understanding of the necessity of storytelling.

About Arif Isikgun

Arif Isikgun has worked with giants such as LVMH, Guerlain, L'Oréal as well as many other well-established independents across the word. With over 17 years of immense experience working in all levels of beauty, luxury retail and spa, launching and educating brands globally. His vision was simple – "Always Innovating Beauty", to innovate emotional connection and empower teams to support not only exceptional client services but brand service also, ensuring full company potential and growth.

His dedicated approach to storytelling was always apparent helping businesses communicate their messages clearly and from a place of emotional intelligence. He founded and launched Ai Beauty Consultancy in 2019 and since has gone on to be an award-winning strategic thinker within education. Speaking at multiple summits and events inspired the power of storytelling and how this can be used as a powerful modern-day tool within education. His tireless work and innovative approach have had transformation results for brands, businesses, hotels and spas helping them achieve record sales and maximise their ability to connect.

Website: www.aibeauty.co.uk

Email: arif@aibeauty.co.uk

Linkedin: www.linkedin.com/in/arifisikgun

Instagram: aibeautyconsultancy

The Heart of Success: Growing My Business With Teamwork And Care

Paula Clipsham

I have been a therapist, a salon owner and an employer for over 30 years.

My top priority is to my team. My team's top priority? Delivering outstanding service and customer care, and genuinely caring about their clients. As Henry Ford said, "It's not the boss who pays the wages, it's the customer."

Positioned over two floors, The Hart Spa is a double fronted, luxurious, five-star, advanced skincare salon. From signing the lease in 1998 on a 3-treatment room basement salon which was only accessible through a hairdressing salon on the ground floor, to coming out of lockdown and taking over the entire ground floor and basement area in April of 2021 and rebranding as "The Hart Spa", it's been an incredible journey, leading to a salon and team I'm extremely proud of. The last three years have been remarkable, even during the most challenging of times, the business has undergone a total transformation.

A full salon refurbishment took place in November 2021, increasing our team from four to nine, increasing our client base by 27% and our overall turnover by 46%. This has definitely proved that team work, shared visions, and client loyalty have been a winning combination for us.

Over the last three years we have been finalists and have won some major awards, including;

- Professional Beauty 2024 Team of the Year – Winner
- Professional Beauty 2024 Large Salon of the Year – Winner
- Professional Beauty 2024 Employer of the Year – Finalist
- Sevenoaks Independent Business of the Year 2023 – Winner
- Professional Beauty 2023 Team of the Year – Winner
- Professional Beauty 2023 Large Salon of the Year – Finalist
- Professional Beauty 2023 Employer of the Year – Finalist
- Muddy Kent Best Beauty Salon in Kent 2022 – Finalist
- Salon of Excellence 2022 – Winner
- Muddy Kent Best Beauty Salon in Kent 2022 – Winner
- Muddy Stiletto's Best Beauty Salon 2022 – Finalist
- Phorest Five Star Customer Experience Award – Awarded for six consecutive years

Winning, and being finalists at these prestigious awards has increased the profile of The Hart Spa, and this increase has had a positive financial impact on the business. Which in turn, has enabled me to ensure job security and long-term careers for the whole team.

My attention is dedicated to my team, spending time with them, reviewing team skills and protocols. I ensure that my whole team stays up to date with the latest treatments and technology, so that they can grow as individuals, and are fulfilled within their careers. Comprehensive training is paramount to me and I invest heavily in my team.

Their skill level is critical to the way we service our clients and how we present ourselves as the most reputable salon in the area.

New employees receive an Employee Handbook and will follow a structured personal training and development program. During the first six to twelve weeks they are mentored by myself and guided by our senior team.

Therapists are guided in treatment techniques and product knowledge to ensure they become experts in all areas of their treatments and aftercare. If relevant, before treatments commence and further professional training is required, this is booked and undertaken by our product partners. This training is reinforced inhouse to ensure they have mastered the correct protocols and to add-on special touches to ensure outstanding treatments and consistency.

I care for every member of my team. Their health, both physical and mental, is paramount to me. If someone is struggling, we work together to manage the issue. I will be as flexible as I possibly can, reducing hours, creating additional breaks, increasing treatment turnaround time and more one to one time with me, are just a few of the examples of what's possible when needed.

I survey the team and hold regular one to ones and team meetings to learn what new treatments excite them, what their dream treatments are and what they would like to offer.

I work with my team. On their 1st anniversary of working at The Hart Spa, the full-time team members have the option of working full time over four or five days per week, some prefer four long days as this gives them an additional day off, others are happy to continue with five days which gives them a couple of early afternoon finishes. I have always offered them this flexibility. Also, after their first year at The Hart Spa they are entitled to one Saturday off a month.

We are a service industry, and Saturdays are a very busy day for us, but it's crucial to me that my team have a work life balance. At present I'm actively recruiting for additional therapists, I would love the whole team to be able have every other Saturday off.

The awards and achievements of the salon since the refurbishment have allowed me to share the success with my team in ways I never thought possible, for example I was able to reward them in October 2022 and October 2023 with an all-expenses paid three day / three night mini break in Spain. This was great for team bonding.

It's important to me that the team bond. We have a great working relationship and the atmosphere in the salon is excellent. This is achieved through regular team building days. The positive financial impact the achievements have made to the business has enabled me close the salon on a regular basis, to hold these team days. Sometimes these are in spa, where we role-play in skin consultations and retail homecare and sometimes we will travel as a team to London to be treated to a one to one training session with the International Institute for Active Ageing (IIAA) our primary industry supplier, who is the UK and Ireland distributor of Environ Skincare, Advanced Nutrition Programme, skin and wellbeing supplements, and et al mineral makeup. Whenever we have team training I always treat them to lunch or dinner to celebrate the team coming together for the day.

The team have individual targets and team targets, rewards for those targets range from products, mini breaks, days and evenings out. We have also had fun awards, "most gushing client review" got some laughs!

We stopped awarding "team player of the month" and "most well-presented". They said it felt wrong to vote for individuals as they are all team players.

I've employed great staff over the last thirty years, and of course it's not always been easy, but I can honestly say this is the best team I've ever had. I have created a friendly, highly skilled and knowledgeable team, who I consider to be some of the best in the industry. We offer incredible treatments and advise on medical grade home-care products, tailoring them to the client's needs, always with outstanding customer service.

Here are just some of the examples of my extraordinary team.

I have a very busy front of house team of four, with two working together each day. Sometimes one will spend long periods of time with a specific client or away from the desk. In June 2022, the team asked if I would pool their retail sales commission and split equally between them, so that if someone was helping a client they wouldn't feel disappointed or discredited at losing a sale. At the time one of the team's retail sales were significantly higher than the others, I later discovered it was her idea. This is a team working together, her generosity and team spirit blew me away.

This is still the case now, even though one has reduced her days for personal reasons, and another increasing hers to help out. They all still pool their retail commission and an equal split is given.

My team are of mixed ages, from 18-55 years old and yet they all get on. They cover holidays/sick days to lessen the impact on the team, and will even swap Saturdays if someone has an event. The team support each other, not just professionally but on a personal level, and it's not unusual to find a team member coming into the salon in their own time to listen or comfort another when they have personal issues, or are having a tough time outside of work.

They often go out of their way to help each other out in the event of travel issues. An example of this was when one of the team picked up and dropped another at home when she fell and hurt her back at the train station, even though this added time onto her journey to work. The same with the train strikes, two come by train and the team have pulled together, making a special effort to ensure everyone could get where they needed to be.

One of the husbands of a team member even offered to picked up a few of the team at 3am and take them home after we landed back from Spain so that I didn't have the additional miles dropping each girl to their homes in the early hours of the morning.

The whole team buy sweets, cakes and biscuits for everyone to share. Our staff room is like a patisserie! They socialise together and loan clothes to each other for evenings out and special occasions. Lynda said it wasn't an option not having everyone at her wedding - they're genuine friends and rarely disagree, that I'm aware of. I can honestly say, I never drive into work wondering what atmosphere I'll be walking into.

My team are just as dedicated to our clients as they are to each other, coming in on days off to do wedding treatments or last-minute specific treatments.

Not only do they support each other, but they give me so much support as well. My team is larger now, team days and holidays are more expensive. They were discussing our trip to Spain on their own WhatsApp chat, and together they decided they would share three to each room, to help reduce the cost of the trip. I was incredibly touched by this.

I'm always asked if there's anything I would do differently, and honestly, there isn't. My greatest achievement is the team I have created. Winning team of the year was incredible.

What do I want to achieve now? No question: Employer of the year! Then I want to continue to speak about nurturing and building teams.

I have always been told I'm so lucky to have such a great team, but luck doesn't really play a part. Nurturing them, listening to them, and genuinely wanting them to be the best they can be, has enabled them to become the team that I am so proud of.

About Paula Clipsham

Paula Clipsham is a speaker, an Advanced Skin Therapist, and the owner of the multi award-winning beauty salon, The Hart Spa, a luxury day spa and beauty salon in the heart of Sevenoaks, Kent. She has one son, Harrison and lives with her two girls, Dee Dee and Nyla, her beloved Toy Cavapoos.

She is passionate about skin health, cherishes her friendships, loves fitness retreats, walking and hiking. Recent adventures include; walking the Inca Trail to Machu Picchu, trekking across the Jordanian desert to Petra, a 9-day trek to Everest Base Camp and spending time at wellbeing and fitness retreats.

Her bucket list includes Kilimanjaro, The Camino de Santiago Pilgrimage and Annapurna Base Camp.

https://thehartspasevenoaks.co.uk

https://www.linkedin.com/in/paula-clipsham-248a1313a/

The Caretaker

Samantha Ashton

There are so many parts to leading a group of people, it's often hard to keep it simple. I have narrowed my key points to four areas: *direction, accountability, approachability* and *problem solving.*

I have titled this chapter, 'The Caretaker', as I have always felt it was my place to support the functions of the department and the people in it, while I was in post in my previous roles. The aim to always ensure I leave a team or department in a better place than when I first arrived.

To write this chapter I asked colleagues and ex employees for feedback on how they felt I was as a leader. I was keen to start with, 'How do I actually lead?' Not the idealistic view in my head. I, personally think that good leaders are made, made from the environment you work in and the people you mix with. In essence the atmosphere we create around our teams (culture).

I have had my biggest successes as a line manager from getting it wrong and having really solid people and training during my early years of managing people. That mix of correct process and human element has made me the manager and hopefully leader that I am today.

Direction

What do you want to achieve? What is needed to get the job done? Whatever the job or task it all starts with an end goal. By having your goals first, you can work backward with what is needed to be achieved by your deadline. Nothing good was ever achieved on your own, you will soon become very busy if you do not delegate to your team.

Once you have your own view of the goal and what is to be achieved you can start to create a visual picture that you will use to communicate and motivate your team to go along on that journey with you.

Knowing your team well really comes alive at this point, I have come to learn that in any role you need to really take your time to get to know your team and your department. I think it's important to have a mix of knowledge about your team skills that you observe, feedback from others and knowing what makes them tick. When I say tick, what motivates them to come to work every day, what do they like and dislike about the role? Knowing them better will allow you to know how to play to their strengths and how do develop them as an individual.

Using this plan or goal allows you to communicate direction and movement. Share what worked well, any learns, or changes needed to that wider plan. In turn celebrating the small steps each day to help you develop security and belonging in the team. Everyone has a place and takes ownership for their part in that goal, finding the direction and movement for themselves to create a sense of purpose and belonging.

This also allows you to resolve any performance issues as you will have a very clear plan for all of your team that you communicate and check in on regularly. In turn creating learning moments and places you can offer support and guidance. This open relationship, I feel, makes individuals come to you when something is not going to plan, asking for support or advice to correct and get back on plan. Having times where individuals can come forward to ask you and the wider peer group for support keeps the team and project moving forward to success. For a plan to work it needs to be dynamic from start to finish.

Accountability

A position with a title can create a feeling of hierarchy within any team. It is needed to create structure in an organisation and is essential, but one I feel is needed to be kept in the background and not the forefront of a team. If I have ever said "you will listen to me because I am your line manager" I have already failed to get that individual on board and contributing.

Establishing an individuals place in the team will give them accountability, belonging, which will help the individual to grow within their team and beyond. We are all adults in the working environment, we all have so much experience, creativity and ideas to bring. By raising accountability as an individual and muting the hierarchy of the job title we create an environment where everyone's input counts. It quickly highlights those that are not contributing, allowing you to have open communication on where and why you feel they are not contributing and what is needed to be changed. This should result in the individual using reflective practices and training to help them understand their contributions matter for the success of the team.

Approachability

Are you approachable? Does your team come to you when it goes right? Do they come to you when it's going wrong? I had always thought I was! However, in a past role I was told by a colleague that when she first met me, she found me scary. I was shocked!

When I asked her why she said I had a direct way to communicate, which she had not had before. Once she got working with me that direct style didn't alter but she saw my personality with it and recognised I had a list and plan and needed her support to get the task completed.

It's often good to pause and ask others how you come across, it can feel scary, but it allows you to adapt your approach and become more approachable.

In any team you need people around you that will question, disagree and challenge why you are doing something a certain way. For a task or goal to truly succeed you need those people around you and you need to ensure you are listening! The key part to being approachable is the knowledge that when they share ideas and challenges you will hear them. That does not mean that you listen to everyone and change the plan but that you will listen, review and decide as the senior leader, does the plan or goal need to change? Can we make it better with these new ideas?

Once an individual has come to you and they see that you have responded well, and the key part is that you listened, this will foster the environment where you are then approachable to your team. Ask them for ideas? Do they think the new roll out plan will work from their point of view?

This is a vital point on any agenda at a team meeting, a space that teams will recognise their area and space to question. Keeping the feedback structured and where all team members can hear it and add to it in a safe structured environment.

Problem Solving

After every half year has completed, I often ask my team to use reflective practice. To look back on the last six months on what they have achieved or still yet to achieve. Time moves so fast it's often difficult to analyse what problems did you face and what did you really do in that moment to over come them?

How have you had to change your plan due to things outside of your control?

I get a great sense of satisfaction on creating a process or a fix for something that's not flowing or working smoothly. That does not mean that I like to change something that isn't broken but to add in structure and really cement ways of working that last even after you are not there. Having your team gain confidence and perspective helps them to manage problems and for them to gain positive emotions around that verses panic or fear. They can then be in a position to navigate through problems and see them as a challenge and not an impossible task. The structure and tools we work to create, allow a freer flowing work environment reducing the extreme situation of daily or even hourly problem solving. Nothing in life is perfect. As a manager or leader, we should be working to reduce problems adding to a calmer holistic working environment.

To summarise my twenty years leading people to success, I have learnt that managing teams and departments is to be myself and go with my gut. Always be yourself!

If a team member doesn't seem themselves, ask them? If a plan needs to change, change it!

Do this with your team getting them on board and involved at every step of the way. Communication is so important and, in my opinion you can never do enough of it. If you think you have communicated the plan, communicate it again in another way, maybe in an email follow up to a meeting. Ensure that you all see the same view and believe in that view.

You will read many books and attend many training sessions on the topic of how to be a leader of people or a good manager, use that only as a guide. The true leader is within us all.

About Samantha Ashton

Samantha Ashton is an experienced sales and education head of department. With over twenty-five years experience in the spa and beauty industry. Ashton began her career qualifying in 1998 as a beauty therapist and aromatherapist. A lifelong passion of scent and skincare began.

Starting as a therapist for Lancôme le Spa, Ashton developed her skills. Moving to spa brand Decleor in 2001 where she moved from being a therapist to her first manager role in 2002.

In 2003, Ashton moved to Estée Lauder brands with Jo Malone London to open store number 8 for the brand. Within twelve months Ashton was the Boutique Manager, leading a large team over a two-year period where they achieved "Store of the Year" for the retail, service and team successes.

Ashton went on to spend thirteen years with Estée Lauder in various roles of Boutique Manager, Education Ambassador, Education Executive and Sales/Education Executive. In 2012, Ashton began her Certificate in Education at Wigan and Leigh College and completing in 2014.

In 2018, Ashton moved to The Hut Group to spend five years with global leading spa brand ESPA. She worked in that period in roles managing teams in sales and training.

2024 sees Ashton move to Irish spa brand Voya. In her spare time, she is a Wife, Mother and runner who loves to crochet.

https://www.linkedin.com/in/samantha-ashton-16a3b396

Just Care More!

Sue Belton

Leading from the heart is actually very simple. Not easy. But simple. It's all about *caring* about and for, the human being(s) in front of you.

As human beings, underneath all of the goals and aspirations, all of the needs and wants, all of the drives and motivations, all we actually want, deep down, is to be loved and to belong.

When you get this, when you know this, and when you come from this place, life and leadership, become a lot simpler.

What's important about this one fundamental truth?

We are *always* relating to another human being. You cannot do or achieve one thing in this life without doing so.

In fact, your survival on this planet depends upon it.

Look what happened to people's mental health during Covid. We are tribal animals, we need others.

Think about it, what's the ultimate punishment dished out by prison institutions and terrorists alike? What's the one, most effective way of breaking people down or making them do or behave in a way that goes against every fibre or moral in their body?

Isolation.

What's important about *Caring* more in leadership.

You can't achieve anything as a leader without people.

I've listened to so many leaders, on our first introductory call, tell me a version of this, being one of the main reasons why they want to do leadership coaching:

"My team just won't do what I say, I just can't make them do what I need them to do, I need to learn how to push them more."

When I ask them: "What have you asked them about what they need? When you've asked about what they might be missing, what they don't have or know in order to complete the task, what have they said?"

They invariably look at me completely puzzled: "What do you mean ask them? Why would I ask them anything, I just need them to do something!"

And there it is.

The one big error I see day in day out in leadership..

People treating people as objects.

A moving piece, to be directed, pushed, told, and then reprimanded (usually publicly, because obviously that will make them more likely not to get it 'wrong' the next time).

Pause, think of a time this happened to you. What was *your* inclination? Did that method make you want to give your all, go above and beyond, and really deliver your best work to help that person achieve *their* goals and objectives?

Pause again.

When did you last behave like that towards someone else?

When did you last see them as a moving part, to be pushed around like a piece on a chess board?

What was the result?

If you want better results, then it's clearly time you get better at relationships, and if you need to do that, you definitely need to start caring more.

How To Start Caring More

1. **Empathy:** Caring leadership begins with empathy.
   It's about stepping into someone's shoes and understanding what someone is going through, acknowledging their struggles, and recognising they are a human being not a human doing!

As a coach, I encourage my clients to step into the shoes of their team members, to imagine the challenges they might be facing, and to consider how it feels to be in a position where they might be perceived as 'failing'. By coming from a place of empathy, leaders can build stronger connections and create environments where individuals feel seen, safe, heard, and valued.

For example, I recently worked with a senior leader who felt highly frustrated with a team member's repeated under performance. Instead of immediately resorting to public criticism (his usual modus operandi), we explored what might be happening in that team member's life that could be affecting their work.

Through this exercise and subsequent implementation, the leader discovered that the team member was struggling with personal issues and needed support rather than punishment. And guess what? Their poor performance stopped almost immediately.

2. **A coaching approach:** Caring leaders understand the importance of coaching and empowering their team members. Instead of always dictating orders, they ask open-ended questions, listen actively, and have meaningful conversations with a view to resolving any challenges. This approach is a win-win all round as it encourages people to be more autonomous, they subsequently grow and develop faster, and it rapidly builds trust within the team.

I coach my clients to ask questions like "What do you need to succeed?" or "What's getting in the way of your progress?" This shifts the focus from command to collaboration, allowing team members to voice their concerns and contribute to finding solutions, so there's also even more buy-in.

By adopting a coaching mindset, leaders are modelling respect for their team members' expertise and insights, which again creates even more engagement

3. **Active listening:** Effective communication is essential for caring leadership. Leaders must not only hear what their team members are saying but also understand the emotions and motivations behind the words. Active listening involves paying attention to verbal and nonverbal cues, empathising with emotions, and responding (instead of unconsciously reacting) thoughtfully.

In coaching sessions, I encourage leaders to practice active listening by paraphrasing, summarizing, and reflecting on what they've heard. By doing so, they demonstrate genuine interest and create a safe space for open dialogue. This creates a mutual understanding, and strengthens the leader-team member relationship even more.

4. **Align with values and purpose:** Caring leaders align their actions with the organisation's values and mission, providing a sense of purpose and direction for their team members. They build commitment by emphasising the greater impact of individual contributions and creating a shared vision that everyone can get onboard with.

As a coach, I help leaders clarify their own values and identify ways to align them with the organisation's goals. We explore questions like "What values drive your leadership style?" and "How can you connect your team's work to the organisation's mission?" By establishing this alignment, leaders cultivate a sense of meaning and belonging among their team members.

5. **Self-ownership:** Caring leadership begins with self-awareness and accountability. Leaders must reflect on their own actions, attitudes, and impact on others, taking full responsibility for creating a supportive and inclusive environment. This requires ongoing self-assessment and a willingness to adapt and improve.

In coaching sessions, I challenge leaders to examine their own role in relationships and outcomes, encouraging them to consider how their behaviour influences others. We explore questions like "Where might you be falling short as a leader?" and "What steps can you take to foster a psychologically safe culture?" By embracing self-ownership, leaders set a positive example and inspire others to do the same.

What *Caring* More Looks Like

A caring leader embodies these principles in their everyday actions and interactions.

They demonstrate empathy by actively listening to their team members' concerns, offering support, and celebrating their successes. They prioritise coaching and development, empowering their team to grow and thrive. They align their leadership with the organisation's values and purpose, inspiring others to contribute meaningfully to shared goals. And they take ownership of their impact, fostering a culture of accountability and continuous improvement.

A caring leader fosters trust, collaboration, and innovation within their team. They create a culture where individuals feel valued, respected, and motivated to achieve their best.

Most importantly, they prioritise people over tasks, recognising that investing in relationships brings long-term success. Ultimately, a caring leader creates an environment where everyone can flourish and fulfill their potential.

What The Future Holds

As we look ahead, caring leadership will become more important than ever before. Millennials, who highly value authenticity, empathy, and purpose, are poised to dominate the workforce and leadership roles. They demand workplaces that prioritise well-being, diversity, and inclusion, and if they don't get it, they'll go elsewhere (or set up on their own).

Caring cultures will become essential for attracting and retaining top talent, driving innovation, and achieving sustainable success. Leaders who do embrace empathy, coaching, active listening, values alignment, and self-ownership will thrive and do well in this new era.

Caring leadership isn't just a nice-to-have—it's a must-have for navigating the complexities of the modern workplace.

By prioritising people, relationships, and purpose, leaders can make a meaningful difference in the lives of their team members, the success of their organisations, and in doing so future-proof their own career and leadership journey…

In conclusion, it makes sense all-round to *just care more.*

About Sue Belton

Sue Belton is a leadership coach who specialises in developing successful leaders who want to be more strategic, influential, and known for making a difference in their industry.

London based, her global clients include established SME Founders, Senior Leaders and C-Level Executives in large multinational companies such as Virgin Wines, Curtis Brown, Costain, and Generali.

She has been awarded Female Entrepreneur of the Year, Best Coach, and was a finalist in the Business Book Awards for her first best selling book *Change Your Life in 5: How to Make Meaningful Changes in Your Life*. Her second book *Screw Meditation! How to Switch Off a Busy Brain, Be More Productive and Enjoy Life!* was also a best seller, and her podcast *Change Makers: Ordinary People Making Extraordinary Changes* has been downloaded in twenty eight countries.

Results-focused, she knows it's win-win: when leaders prioritise and focus on their own development, they and their teams are happier and more fulfilled, perform better, have happier clients, and get better results for the business.

Website: *www.suebelton.com*

LinkedIn: *https://www.linkedin.com/in/suebelton/*

Email: sue@suebelton.com

Leading From The Heart, With Purpose...

Tabitha James-Kraan

I grew up in a small village in Worcestershire, the eldest daughter of five children. Life was pretty idyllic; we spent a lot of time outside playing in nature and having simple freedoms that allowed our imaginations to run wild. We were surrounded by animals and had ponies to play with, as well as to fall off, which is how we learnt to ride them. My sisters and I would push the cats and kittens around in our little prams and play like little mummies, busy staying out of the house once we had all done our chores.

We were loved, safe and happy, we mostly ate the food that my parents grew in their garden and the fowl that roamed in the small plot of land that was cultivated to fit the "good life" that my parents wanted to achieve. This was all organic living before organic was a thing... Mainly of course because it was then just called growing food.

When we moved to the village dad befriended the locals who grew vegetables on their allotments, he learnt how to grow smartly without using pesticides, instead growing plants alongside each other to keep the various bugs from eating the food. Similarly to what I later learnt is the bases for biodynamic farming, it is funny how you can see the beginnings of your interests in your childhood.

I left school at 16 and started an apprenticeship in hairdressing. My Mum had been a hairdresser before starting a large family and I recently discovered that my grandmother had also been a hairdresser. Now my son has also trained and qualified in the industry, making him the fourth generation to do so. I had originally set out to be a chef and was definitely not going to be a hairdresser as my memory was the horrible perm chemicals that my mum had occasionally exposed us to when perming an elderly aunt's hair. It was not until I saw the knives that I needed to use in the butchery department as part of the chef's education that I did a full 360 and found myself an apprenticeship as a hairdresser in Stratford-upon-Avon. One week into this I was in love, I loved the creativity, the possibilities and doing all of that with so many human interactions - it was joyous from day one and I still love those aspects of it today.

Fast forward to 1993, I opened the doors to my first hair salon with a loan from the Princes Youth Business Trust. I was young and hungry for success and determined to build the best salon outside of London, it was going to have a team all trained in London, bring the best practice and shake up the Cotswolds.

In 1999, I found my purpose! This started when I became pregnant with my first child and a conversation with a savvy midwife changed the course of my life…

She told me to stop colouring my hair because the colour would absorb into my bloodstream via my hair follicles and would travel into my unborn child, a fact that stopped me in my tracks. Nobody in my industry had ever told me this before, none of the immense studying I had done, none of the books I had read, none of the educational courses I had taken. I was shocked to my core, not just because of my pregnancy but the idea that what I was doing in my day job was affecting the bodies of those that I was working on.

I bring joy to people through my work, I make them look

good, feel good about themselves but now I also recognised that I could be doing something that might also cause harm. I had a lightbulb moment from which I couldn't turn back, there had to be another way to do this, I was just going to have to find it.

My team thought I had gone mad at first, so did most of the people in the Cotswold village of Broadway when they walked past the salon and saw the sign "Organic Hairdressing". In the summer months with the doors open I would hear people saying, "organic hairdressing, blimey I have heard it all now, whatever next?". It didn't stop there, some of my team kicked back at me and left as it was too much of a change to go out on a limb into such unchartered territory. They found it hard, as I had literally changed everything about what we were using in the salon, from the health store hair care I found, to the strict rules on what we would use to colour hair and how we would apply it. This involved running in the opposite direction to my whole industry for a while and navigating unchartered waters.

Leading By Example

Fast forward again to 2015. I took my purpose to the next level, I knew that there were only so many people that I could reach through my Cotswold salon. There was literally a whole world out there to share the love with by sharing the good news that there were better ways to work in my wonderful industry, not involving being so harmful to our health and the health of the planet. A way of working towards a sustainable future for hairdressing.

I had now learnt so much and had so much to share about how to work differently as a hairdresser. My team and I had developed a sustainable best practice and it was working. bI needed a vehicle to extend the reach of this new philosophy…

I had still not found the products that I wanted to work with in my salon, everything I found was telling a good story, the marketing was everything I was looking for but it was greenwashing. So there was only one thing for it, I was going to have to make them myself.

I spent years leading up to this point visioning and playing with raw ingredients in my kitchen, until I found what I needed to go to the labs and start my own range of Certified organic hair care. I found a way to look differently at how we were washing hair in the first place, going right back to basics. Why do we use a degreasant that is designed to remove all traces of oil from the hair and the scalp? I know that this creates chaos in the body as it strips the natural protective layer from the skin, the "acid mantle" and our very clever bodies then work hard to put it back, creating a greasy scalp or hair that needs washing again. I knew I had to change this approach and do something differently, I had to make something that could enable the hair to be washed less, ultimately to use less water and also less carbon heating the water each year of use.

I was going to have to create a method that would support the body in a different way and still meet the needs of hairdressers, as well as the needs of our end consumers – the hair washing public that the products needed to reach.

There had to be a very good reason to make yet another hair care product to go to market, I knew that the products would have to have strong values that would lead by example.

- I knew they would have to be authentically free from synthetic ingredients that over-stimulate our bodies, often containing endocrine disruptors that cause hormonal issues and a host of other negative effects. Instead natural ingredients that could work in balance and in harmony with us.

- The provenance became paramount, I understood that if we are taking from nature, we need the best quality ingredients for potency and efficacy and the best way to achieve this is organic and biodynamic ingredients. So they needed to be grown organically without the use of herbicides and pesticides and chemical fertilisers in order to protect biodiversity. To support organic farming generally for the future of our soil, we need to be respectful of what we are taking and how that process works in practice, what do we leave behind, is it sustainable to take the ingredients, how does it affect the soil?

- That we needed to understand the impact of the products themselves from what was being washed into our water systems to what happens to the packaging once we have it in our possession.

- This lead to a whole new way of working with clients in salon to, one that is more about self empowerment through making educated, conscious choices.This also incorporates looking at everyone as an individuals and their health and wellness. Focussing on bringing out everyone's inner beauty and not imposing the current obsession with perfection that our society is fixated on. When a person looks in the mirror and smiles because they feel good in the skin they are in. We see beauty in that smile, and happiness in their eyes.

To conclude, I had to find a way to change what I had discovered back in 1999, to ensure that we, as an industry, could work in a way that allowed us to wash hair less, colour hair less and have less impact on the planet in the way that we work as hairdressers.

By 2017, I was selling the range to salons and stores in 20 separate countries around the world, speaking and educating along the way.

The products have gained over 30 awards and I was honoured to receive a PEA award for "green pioneer", as well as reaching the top 10 of "Who's Who in natural beauty."

I was now embarking on the journey of my life's work to educate hairdressers and the public on how to use less to get more when it comes to our hair and how we look after it.

In 2021, I joined the Sustainable Beauty Coalition for the British Beauty Council and started work with a taskforce that supports hair and beauty salons as well as spa's. I am currently working with industry bodies to develop qualifications for sustainability within the hair & beauty sector to empower young people coming into the profession with knowledge to prepare and hopefully inspire them to keep improving the status quo.

Even after all this time, I feel like I am just getting started and I'm revelling in the current landscape as there is now such a huge movement for change. I truly believe in the power of humanity to ultimately get us where we need to be. My love of nature has always been at the heart of all that I have done in my work and how I live my life day-to-day, it is the first thing I love to share to connect with others.

Sometimes leadership isn't necessarily just about 'telling'. For me, 'leadership' can be running in the opposite direction to everyone else, leading by example to show others a new way, and ultimately encouraging them to join you on an exciting and fulfilling journey of discovery.

About Tabitha James-Kraan

Tabitha JK - The organic hair pioneer, has been delivering her brand of conscious hairdressing since 1993.

As well as her Cotswold Organic hair salon, Tabitha has pioneered a professional, organic hair care range, (Tabitha James Kraan hair organics), that is certified by the Soil Association (Cosmos Organic).

Tabitha is a public speaker, blogger and influencer in the natural beauty sector. Tabitha is an advisory board member for the Hair Task Force for the British Beauty Council's Sustainability Coalition. Tabitha is also on the advisory board for noon.org. In her own words Tabitha is a "Hair Geek" , a passionate naturalist, environmentalist, animal lover, spirited horsewoman, all round organic guru and Queenager.

https://tabitha-jameskraan.com

https://www.instagram.com/tabithajk/

https://www.linkedin.com/in/tabithajk/

The Qualities That Count

Jessica Parrish

The idea of telling my story regarding leadership, initially makes me question myself and why I am being asked to contribute; and to really consider my leadership style. Of course, imposter syndrome kicks in: I query what I have to offer and this in turn forces me to take a step back...

- I have over 20 years' experience, working and leading in business.
- I have an MBA from Cranfield University – one of the best when it comes to leadership.
- I have launched and now run my own successful business. Shedid & Parrish, a premium, natural, hair range for curly and textured hair.

So, in retrospect, maybe I do know a thing or two about leading both from an academic - theoretical sense and in practice.

Personally, I'm fascinated by people. What makes people tick, what makes them behave the way they do, what influences decision-making, what drives the best results. As individuals we all carry so much around with us - our hopes, dreams, and aspirations but equally emotional baggage from our childhood, family pressures and expectations which influence how we function.

Not everyone wants the same thing out of their work and lives. Some people are happy to complete a task, not get engaged and shut down at the allotted finish time; others need to understand the whole picture and how their portion of work contributes to the wider whole and fundamentally care about the various elements at play. To understand this and who feels what, at the heart of it all from the perspective of a leader is listening: being mindful of who makes up the team, how they operate and what they need to be their best selves. The best leaders inspire but equally, and perhaps more importantly, take the time to understand their people to really support their needs and by doing so getting what the business needs. With this mindset a leader can build a profitable and happy business environment.

I remember working in one of my corporate companies, where we were part of what I would now see as a rather old-fashioned leadership style. It was traditionally male, aggressive, and hierarchical. Interestingly, the women often became even hyper masculine and aggressors as a way to compete successfully in this space. The premise was that friction would create competition and with competition comes growth. Whilst there is certainly a place for this style of culture and leadership, it also stifles. It doesn't allow the quieter contributors to speak up, nor support collaboration cross functionally. Whilst it could be argued that it creates solidarity – Us vs Them – it is not so good when Us *and* Them could work together to deliver much more beneficial outcomes. The end result was the loudest of management rode high and the majority of everyone else became disenfranchised as they were never going to be in that dominant position which ultimately bred resentment.

In this environment, I was labelled 'soft' and seen as not 'aggressive enough'.

I had to question my behaviors, how I best functioned, and what I was comfortable with. Yet despite those criticisms, I often achieved better results and built and maintained more cohesive and collaborative relationships with both colleagues and clients alike.

My style, then and now, has always been more collaborative. I subscribe to the win-win philosophy. Of course, in negotiation they say that this is a misnomer. There's a win and win more, but if all parties feel heard and believe they have won on the terms that matter to them, then really everyone has won.

Once I got into a position of leadership and became responsible for others, I found that certain qualities were paramount: Compassion, Authenticity, and Passion.

Compassion

Compassion isn't just about seeing people, who they are and empathising with how those around you feel, it's the desire to help too where needed. Our people, our teams are not just colleagues and staff, they are humans with their own interests, behaviours, and distractions. Leading from the Heart with compassion considers the needs of those around you so that they can be their best selves. It's about listening to their needs and empowering them to operate at their best. Supported in the right way our people are our greatest assets.

In previous environments I've worked in, success was assessed through being present, where you are physically at your desk at a particular moment in time. I think that the COVID pandemic has actually helped reshape this notion. Rather than an employee being measured by being seen sat at their desk, it became more about their output. I recall way back when, one of our CEOs morphed himself onto this kind of robot that would prowl the office and he'd be watching from the safety of his own office (or even home!).

He could see who was there without actually interacting properly with anyone but would still judge based on presence and of course he did those tours early or late in the day. This not only bred fear, but also resentment and a culture of not feeling trusted. If you're deemed untrustworthy you may as well behave as expected.

As a Leader, I come from the perspective that people want to do a good job, they want that pat on the back and to obtain recognition and approval as much as many seek to learn and grow. I have found that by investing time, encouragement, and education, where needed, leads to loyalty and retention and a desire for team members to want to continue working with you. In addition, when the leader displays compassion for others, it sends a message to the rest of the team to treat their colleagues with the same consideration. The supportive learning, sharing skills and, celebrating each other becomes the culture and these qualities are reflected amongst the team.

Authenticity

The quality of being genuine and real and true to who you are and what you do. Leading with authenticity isn't always easy. It means being vulnerable and transparent but with this also comes a strength. As a leader, being authentic requires honesty and owning up to mistakes and failings. But as there are no lies, there is nothing to hide behind, and nothing to incorrectly remember. There is a defined direction of travel, and the team can clearly see the path. As a young business I have learnt that without failure it is very difficult to grow, it means you're not trying hard enough. Encouraging such a culture amongst one's team enables a safe space where people feel able to contribute and that learning from failure is a key growth tool. By leading authentically, the team are part of all the experiences both good and bad. They feel the pain and disappointment when things go wrong but can truly celebrate the successes and own them as part of their own journey making them feel all the sweeter.

Passion

When leading a business, I believe that passion is paramount. It is the uncompromising drive and vision that pushes us forward and enables others to follow and be part of the journey. As a leader, I have been uncompromising in my passion and drive when it comes to my business Shedid & Parrish. Our values are what sets us apart; a brand that is as considerate to the environment as it is to our hair; a brand that uses only the finest ethically sourced ingredients for the best hair health and a brand that is truly inclusive of all curl patterns, having been formulated carefully for the tightest coil to loosest wave. This passion drives our brand pillars and becomes a reflective mirror to be held up against everything we do.

It isn't easy, particularly in a very overcrowded market where around 600 new beauty products are launched every year and financial success is derived by how much marketing budget is available. But our passion is what sets us apart and keeps us focused and consistent. Financial profitability is of course inherent to what we do but how we deliver that profit is just as important and the passion sitting behind that keeps us true and honest.

This passion has helped us cut through. It has led us to build some wonderful partnerships with other brands and individuals who hold the same values and are relentless in pursuit of doing business ethically and with purpose. This passion has inspired team members to want to work with us for the sheer experience rather than the financial reward and it has enabled us to become multi award winning from an early age by the industry bodies.

Putting people first and Leading from the Heart in my experience leads to not only a successful business but also a profitable one. When everyone on the team believes in the business, they will often put in the same level of focus and drive to make it a success. That's a team driving the business forward, not just the founder.

I believe in positive energy, in putting out to the universe what you wish to receive. By Leading from the Heart with *Compassion, Authenticity* and *Passion*, your people and those you surround yourself with can be your greatest assets. The business success is wonderful but so too is the journey and seeing others develop and grow along the way. Equally, seeing the business develop in ways you may not have foreseen had your team not been empowered to take it forward is very humbling. Leading is a privilege and seeing how your influence touches others is truly rewarding particularly knowing that the shared experience has such positive benefits for those you touch in more ways than purely financial.

About Jessica Parrish

Jessica is a senior executive with over 20 years of commercial experience working across the UK, Europe, North America and the Middle East. From 2021 she launched and runs the award winning premium hair range for curly and textured hair; Shedid & Parrish.

She has mixed heritage of Sudanese, Italian, Congolese and Belgian ethnicity and was adopted into a white British, Canadian family in the suburbs of London. Having struggled with identity from a young age, by being 'other' she developed the ability to cross social groups and put people first.

She launched Shedid & Parrish to battle against the hair discrimination that still exists, providing a formulated range for all curl patterns.

She now speaks about hair equity which includes the importance of understanding various hair textures, the hair discrimination that is still experienced and how to eradicate it.

Her product range is now used by some of the leading curl academies, stars of stage and screen, and curlies worldwide.

https://shedidandparrish.co.uk

https://www.linkedin.com/in/jessicaparrishuk

https://www.linkedin.com/company/shedid-parrish-ltd

https://www.instagram.com/shedidandparrish

https://www.facebook.com/shedidandparrish

https://www.tiktok.com/@shedidandparrish

Leadership Through Passion And Self Care

Clare Porter

Discovering my leadership style

What an honour and privilege it is to be asked to participate in a book was my thought when I was invited to contribute to Leading from the Heart.

Initially I spoke to my husband and asked "But do I lead from the heart?" He replied instantly. "Definitely! You care so much and are always moving forward." Then I mentioned my doubts to one of my team who replied. "I think it's probably because it comes so naturally to you."

A friend exclaimed: "Absolutely. You're such an inspiration. You're enthusiastic, you're passionate, and you've got so much knowledge". Then a client shared with me the significant value she has found in her treatments over the past few months, especially during a challenging period. She expressed how the breathing techniques I suggested had been effective for her.

Hearing this made me realise that I *do* lead from the heart. I just hadn't thought about it like that before. I suppose it's because it feels a little bit disingenuous, because actually, I love what I do.

It's not just a job. I have created an environment that is built from a passion and understanding of what we can offer as a beauty salon.

I've been a beauty therapist for nearly 33 years now and I'm still in treatments most days. I often call my treatment room my happy place as I find it so rewarding. It's an amazing industry to be in.

Now, I have a big heart, and I'm inherently kind. I love everything. I love helping and caring for people. I love doing things that bring joy and happiness. I love listening to people's different experiences and travels. I love dancing and singing. I love to be busy and fulfilled. I love to smile and live a purposeful life. I am enthusiastic with a thirst for knowledge. I'm focused when it comes to seeking opportunities to expand my expertise and skills. There's also an energy that's fuelled by this passion and confidence which also makes me a strong character - Some have even said a force! I can be a little bit too much of a Pollyanna sometimes with my optimism but I recognise these things about myself and I have found a balance where I can be the person I like and love.

Self Reflection And Personal Growth

During a yoga class, at a bit of a challenging time in my life, I discovered the importance of taking care of my own well being and my big heart.

Despite appearing capable on the surface, a yoga teacher encouraged me to sit still, breathe deeply and place my hands over my heart. I wasn't prepared for what followed. It was out of the blue for me. I was completely overwhelmed by tears, uncontrollable tears, and it became evident that I was neglecting my own needs while pouring all of my energy into various aspects of my life.

It took me some time to acknowledge that I truly wasn't okay, and that I was running on empty. Every time for weeks that I put my hand on my heart I would cry again and I was giving myself a hard time about it! Eventually I realised I was constantly giving to others without considering my own well being.

It was a wake up call. After a strong conversation with myself, I made a plan to tailor my own self care routine so that I could still be the caring person I am, but make certain there was something left for me. Basically, practice what I was preaching to my clients, friends and team and take some time to be kind to myself.

So now I have a daily routine where I meditate first thing in the morning. After feeding the cat, I get on my mat and do some yoga. When considering admin tasks for my day ahead I always aim to conquer the item I dread most first, as that way the day can only get better! These simple daily steps bring me balance and align with my true self.

So, that is enough about me. I felt it relevant to provide some insight into the true values and building blocks of the beauty salon I have today. We are a team of six, two of which are apprentices, and we have an extremely loyal clientele and a reputation for excellence.

Team Values And Practices

"Do what you love. Love what you do" is the quote in our staff room.

The first thing I ask when interviewing is "What made you want to be a beauty therapist?" I like to hear their story of why. The amount of times I hear the passion as they explain how they take pride in their treatments or the variety of treatments they can offer. It is important to me to work with likeminded people. We have designed our salon so that people want to come in and enjoy treatments and the time spent here - whether that be for a client or a therapist. Additionally I aim to create an environment where my team enjoy coming to work.

We have regular staff meetings and all of the team are encouraged to contribute ideas and help find solutions. We all support each other throughout the day, whether that be turning rooms around or welcoming the next client with a smile. I regularly have one to ones with every member of the team and do hope that everyone knows that I am always here to support them.

We make time to discuss and ensure everyone understands our core ethos and values and I trust my team to all work together to achieve this. If we ever do get a negative review or comment I express to the team that actually for someone to take the time to feedback to us then they want us to improve. This can be a compliment, after all we want to offer the best possible experience for our clients and by having these insights we can learn and improve. It is always about how you deal with a problem that is most important.

Having apprentices has been both rewarding and empowering for the whole team. You forget how much you know until you start sharing your knowledge and expertise and overall it has created a learning environment throughout the salon.

Empowering Excellence

A question I have recently asked at interview is regarding if there is anything that has made therapists feel stuck in their career.All too often this falls down to training which is something I really pride myself and the salon on. I love this quote from Richard Branson and I think he has it spot on.

"Train people well enough so that they can leave, treat them well enough so that they don't want to" - Richard Branson

I love to learn, it is something that is so fabulous about the industry as it constantly evolves so there is always something new to learn. Giving my team opportunities to flourish and expand their treatment repertoire and skill set is fundamental to our core values. Our whole team is fully trained with all of our brands, we do refreshers regularly and also regularly update our treatment list accordingly. It keeps us all motivated to grow and keeps us interested. I welcome any suggestions too and we have regular promotions where treatment combinations are created by our therapists. I like us all to remember that we are experts. This is something we don't champion enough.

Through regular communication our team are empowered to excel in their roles and contribute to the success of the salon. As the business continues to grow, so too does my commitment to nurturing the professional growth of my team. Each team member deserves to feel valued, supported, and inspired to reach their full potential. It's a privilege to be able to be part of that journey.

Philosophy Of Wellness In The Salon

I like our therapists to experience the benefits of our treatments firsthand. The power of touch is widely acknowledged and one of our brands has recently studied the beneficial effects with impressive results. Prioritising wellness is crucial in our role as therapists and fundamental for nurturing the well being and performance of our team and salon as a whole.

We regularly take time within the salon to discuss various self care techniques and I encourage the team to carve out moments for themselves each day. It is all too easy to be consumed by the doing and neglect our own needs. We also share these practices with our clients, whether it is through breathing exercises, meditation or simply being fully present.

As beauty therapists we embody kindness and care in our daily role but it is equally important for us to prioritise self care. I am careful not to overly emphasise positivity, allowing therapists the space to reflect on their day comfortably. Sometimes, we absorb a lot from our clients and it is essential to prevent overwhelming feelings from accumulating. I can't help but think of the Pixar film Inside out when I talk to the team about this.

In Summary

I realise now that I am indeed Leading from the Heart and I feel very grateful to be in a career that enables me to do that. When I sit with my self and place my hands on my heart nowadays I have a feeling of immense pride. I have the privilege of working with some amazing people and have so many opportunities and experiences to be thankful for. This has all been achieved through authenticity, passion, a love of learning and having a big heart.

About Clare Porter

Clare is a dedicated salon owner with over 30 years of experience as a beauty therapist. Specialising in massage and facials. She is continuously learning and evolving to provide the best treatment every visit.

Clare is honoured to have co-authored "Beauty and the Best 2," inspiring beauty professionals, and is a Lemonista with Know Your Lemons, advocating for breast health. Recently Clare has also trained in The Spurgeon Massage, a bodywork protocol beneficial for the upper torso, including the breast, to relieve pain, reduce oedema and increase range-of-motion.

As a Judge for Professional Beauty and an ambassador for Apprenticeships with HABIA, Clare's commitment to the industry drives her. Her passion and knowledge shine through in every aspect of her work.

When not in a treatment room Clare has a love of the outdoors, a penchant for travel, a daily yoga practice and will usually be wearing a dress!

www.fountainbeauty.co.uk

Heart-Led Education

Diane Hey

Heart-Led Education...

My career in the beauty, spa and wellbeing industry began as an enthusiastic, slightly overwhelmed Spa therapist, eager to prove myself and progress! Looking back what a journey! I have seen and experienced various roles and styles of leadership, some I wouldn't want to emulate and some where I have taken on board valuable lessons which have informed my methods and style of working.

I'm best known for education in my career, leading various Government developments and creating pathways and architectural structures to enable employment ready routes for entrants into our industry in the UK, alongside leading a business (which I'm less well known for) in wellbeing, beauty therapy and spearheading spa apprenticeships. This is more to me than just a job, I feel it is incumbent to continuously upskill our workforce and bring forward the next generation of thinking therapists and leaders. It allows me to put something back, to an industry that has provided me with such richness and opportunity, colleagues and friends.

Empowering Growth Through Education

Where to start with my own leadership, am I a leader or a facilitator of growth for those I interact with, in this main role? Leadership to me is very much built on the authentic human connections created, building trust and respect, which needs to be earnt as a leader, not a given because you hold the title. I've always worked on the basic principle of never expecting anyone to do something I wouldn't, haven't or don't still do.

Education to me is a journey of empowerment and growth, that lasts a lifetime, I firmly believe both as a business leader and educator (learning leader) in providing opportunities for development, equipping our teams and learners with the knowledge, skills, behaviours and **confidence** to excel, not just in their job roles but in 'life'. Managing classrooms of learners as a dual professional in my days in further education and early teaching career, was one very sure way of helping me develop an empathic and nurturing approach, learners would soon vote with their feet if you got it wrong or would just switch off, just because you were leading the class, didn't mean they had to listen, much like leading a team, you have to ignite engagement and maintain it!

I learnt that explanation, bringing everyone on the journey and sharing some professional anecdotes of things I learnt whilst working helps, letting others see that I had developed and made mistakes, that I wasn't born ready to lead and am still learning, allowed me to create cultures where all are valued and value each other. I've established a style of openness to listen whilst also setting clear boundaries, standards of behaviour and professional etiquette for the working environment and expectations, being able to make tough decisions with conviction and the backing of my teams.

The greatest gift for me to give as a leader is time, I've seen and cringed over many years, when I've heard and hear it said

'I haven't got time' which translates to a team member or learner who is seeking guidance as *'you or your issue is not important enough for me to make time for'*, it's a most valuable gift, caring enough to invest in making a meaningful difference to an issue of importance to your team, is paramount to building empathy and trust. We all have a bad day!

Resilience And Emotional Intelligence

Building emotional resilience and emotional intelligence has never been more important, back to making authentic connections. We all have differing value systems, driven by varying life factors and experience, listening to my team and making time for conversations allows me to understand what matters to them, what are their motivators, their why for what they do. It is important to understand that our different life journeys and opportunities affect how we approach situations, meaning as leaders we need to not impose our own thinking but acknowledge each team members individuality and pathway. Over time and being embedded in the company values and leading by example supports my team to evolve.

We spend quite a bit of time with our team to learn how to reflect and critic their own work, being self-aware to self-assess, separating the process from the personal, which is possibly one of the hardest aspects to learn and embed, it's hard not to see things as personal, particularly in roles where we have so much scrutiny in terms of audit and compliance, yet when achieved it is a great skill set. It gives time to help understand their emotions, celebrate their strengths and identify any improvements which in turn builds resilience to the knocks we can be subject to working with the public, in regulated education and one that possibly took me the longest to acquire and still improving, in the pursuance of excellence!

We explore how stress impacts performance, what is stressful to one team member might not be to another or vice versa, stress being pertinent to the individual. We've expanded our base of mental health first aid access, in addition to life coaching skills acquired early in my career continuing my own continual development, discussing coping strategies for all, celebrating the positive to cultivate gratitude and optimism, whilst also being realistic about the challenges which may be being faced. Where signposting and greater support is needed, it is sourced, offered and accessed.

Resilience without doubt requires adaptability, individually and as a team, finding solutions together that might not be perfect but allows sufficient positive change to minimise any setbacks. It also builds confidence in our practice of our operating procedures which has become a process of continuous improvement, setting our intent, implementation and review on a continuum. It grasps opportunities and permits growth for the business and team success!

Patience, Open Minded

I am naturally quite an impatient leader which I've observed most are, driven and proactive, driving forward. However, working in my chosen fields including with Governments and Boards has taught me patience and to keep an open mind. The outcomes to seek the best solutions within frameworks that can sometimes appear restrictive, can take a long time to evolve ideas (Policy), patience is essential to being inclusive to ensure industry voices are heard and the outcomes deliverable, but also a huge privilege to be the conduit with my peers.

Why?

To me my roles are also about my social responsibility to make the world a better place, touching lives, giving opportunities, removing barriers and making a difference with kindness and compassion, whilst prioritising values and nurturing a culture of transparency, collaboration and trust in all my interactions. In turn enabling greater fulfilment, success and recognition for those we work with in all aspects of my work and life.

About Diane Hey

Diane Hey, Founder & CEO of Armonia Health and Wellbeing, holds over 35 years' experience in spa and wellbeing industries. She's renowned as an industry expert, focusing on apprenticeships and professional training in spa, beauty, wellbeing and aesthetics. In 2000, she launched Armonia Health and Wellbeing, including Armonia Training Academy, an Ofsted-rated, Government-approved education provider.

For over 25 years, Diane has championed employment-ready education, collaborating with various UK Government initiatives and departments to uphold standards. As a technical advisor, she works with all UK National educational regulators, holding key advisory roles and Chair positions.

Diane is dedicated to setting standards, evident in her role as a Trustee for Standards Authority for Touch in Cancer Care (SATCC). Additionally, she Chairs the National Occupational Standards for Hair and Beauty Industry Authority (Habia) reviews and serves as a BABTAC Board member, committed to elevating wellness sector standards. Diane focuses on regulated educational pathways, fostering talent pipelines and sustainable career development. Her exceptional contributions were recognized with the Industry Beyond Award in September 2023.

Careers@armonia.co.uk

www.linkedin.com/in/diane-hey-31190583

People First Leadership

Jen Buck

I remember when I started my career at 18 years old, bright eyed and full of optimism. I was a college student without a completed degree, without an appropriate corporate wardrobe, and absolutely without any experience beyond waitressing. Yet, somehow, I was miraculously hired by this startup. I had no idea of what to expect from the corporate world but I knew that I wanted to be there and learn as much as I could.

This startup environment was supercharged, motivating, and full of fun… ultimately, the entire vibe was about keeping the employees inspired and excited. They were employee-focused to the absolute max and bent over backward to make sure that the employee base was feeling valued and recognized, all the time. We knew that our opinions and input mattered. We knew that they were grateful for our commitment to the mission. We knew that they were invested in our success. And, while we weren't the highest paid workers on the block, we certainly felt like we were the most appreciated. Looking back over my ten years with the company, I know that this was the foundation that has since become the true north of my leadership style and subsequent branding of my corporate training.

The reason that startup became an award-winning, globally recognized, and industry disrupting brand (which is in the Fortune 50 to this day) is found in their commitment to their employees' well-being.

They didn't have a product that was especially unique. They didn't have an idea that had never been heard of. What they had was a desire to get a piece of the pie in their industry, and brought in an incredibly tenacious commitment to valuing people, which insured they would be able to reach their goal. And, boy did they ever reach that goal!

I have spent the last 25 years of my career as a Professional Speaker teaching organizations how to create that same kind of environment for their employees. I call it *People First Leadership* and it starts at the top of the organization.

That People First commitment is what will create momentum on the front lines and guaranteed success in the long run. It's what will keep the excitement and commitment alive in the employee base because they are consistently recognized. It's what will allow them to experience longevity in their brand because they limit, and often decrease, their turnover. When a leadership team puts the majority of their focus on rewarding, recognizing, praising, and exciting their people – and takes themselves out of the equation - you start to see a groundswell of joy, loyalty, increased profits, delighted clients, and personal leadership success. The hard part is getting leaders to take themselves out of the equation and trust that their personal success will come from putting People First. And, I promise you that personal success comes.

I had the great privilege of working with SAS in North Carolina and I was blown away at the extraordinarily happy people and incredible campus. Driving on to the campus for the first time reminded me more of a university environment than a business campus. There were people playing catch with a football, groups sitting under trees chatting, people riding bikes, and even a kickball game happening... and all of this was in the middle of the morning during working hours. I didn't know what to make of what I was witnessing, but I recognized something familiar on the faces that I was studying: JOY. These people were full of excitement, optimism and inspiration and I was immediately taken back to the first decade of my career at the startup. It was the same feeling and vibe, and it hit me like a ton of bricks. I got it… I recognized it… I felt it.

And, clearly SAS got it; they're a People First organization. They've received the Best Place to Work Award several times throughout the last two decades and have a 5% annual turnover, which is extraordinary. Provided on their campus, all employees get to enjoy these types of benefits:

- Hair, nail, and massage salon
- Free healthcare and pharmacy onsite
- Free childcare and a primary school
- A world-class gym and pool. And an expectation that you will work out for one hour of your 8-hour day
- Unlimited sick days
- Maternity and paternity leave
- Car service station
- Shipping center
- Six cafes with options from sushi to pizza

Dr. Goodnight is the CEO of SAS and an extraordinary example of a People First Leader. I remember sitting in a line to leave the campus and I noticed that there was a man standing at the guard gate waving at each car as they passed through at the end of their day. When it was my turn at the gate, I learned that the gentleman was Dr. Goodnight. This man alone is responsible for creating the incredible environment that the employees get to experience, day in and day out. He is the reason why they have the best buffet of munchies in every work area, prized art on every wall, beautiful environments to work within, and a laundry list of out of this world benefits. He gets it.

I found out that Dr. Goodnight can be found at the gate every single night, waving at each car and wishing them well at the end of their day. He's been quoted as saying, "Every night, 95% of my assets drive out of the gate —it's my job to keep them coming back."

That is People First Leadership in action.

Being a People First Leader is having an over-arching commitment to recognizing and valuing your employees continually, which aligns with modern expectations of workplace culture. In today's competitive job market, attracting and retaining top talent requires more than just competitive salaries. Job satisfaction, which includes feeling appreciated and valued, is a significant factor for employees when choosing and staying with an organization. People First Leaders understand that it's not an option to mostly-sort of-kind of-partially commit to this way of leading—you have to go all in. It's committing to putting recognition first and making it your biggest priority.

What we know about human behavior is that recognition is the key to a person's heart. Freely sharing kindness and appreciation is what transforms individuals. For too long we have seen Transactional Management poisoning our workforce and sadly it still permeates some of the hallways. In its simplest terms Transactional Management styles are recognized as, "If you're nice to me, I'll be nice to you. If you go out of your way for me, I'll go out of my way for you" types of behaviors.

The thing is, that's an outdated managerial style that has long passed it's due date. Transactional relationships never, ever work and it's time for them to be put out to pasture.

The most renowned leaders understood the power of recognition and value. Jack Welch of GE knew the personal details of the employees who worked for him. He inquired about kid's baseball game scores, family member's surgery outcomes, and vacation plans. It didn't matter if you were a c-suite member or part of the sanitation team, Jack Welch made it his mission to value and engage with every person. Richard Branson of Virgin knew that people had to feel like they were genuinely being seen, heard, and taken care of, which is reflected in the decades long tenure that his employees have with his organization. More recently, we see leaders like Jeff Weiner, the CEO of LinkedIn, creating a corporate value around Compassion. He believes that being compassionate is not just a better way to build a team, it's a better way to build a company. Weiner says that compassionate leadership is about taking action and helping your employees feel better. Another thing that makes him such a great leader is that he devotes 90 minutes of his time every day to coaching and spontaneous conversations with his co-workers.

Author John Maxwell said, "People will jump through hoops, walk over hot coals, and follow you to the ends of the earth, if they know you love them." While I'm not looking for you to profess your love to your employees and get yourself in hot water with HR, I am telling you that your people need to see, hear, and experience that you genuinely care and are putting their morale and wellbeing at the top of your priority list.

That's how People First Leaders do it.

People First Leaders understand that the commitment to employee recognition and value has a profound impact on their own personal leadership success.

While it may seem like one more thing to add to your to-do list, or another fad leadership theory to adopt, the truth is that it's been the secret of the most beloved and heralded leaders in our modern business history.

People First Leadership is essential because it addresses the evolving needs and expectations of the workforce, promotes employee well-being, adapts to changing work environments, fosters diversity and inclusion, and contributes to organizational success in a rapidly evolving and interconnected world. Leaders who prioritize people create environments where individuals can thrive, leading to enhanced productivity, innovation, and overall organizational resilience. Investing in the well-being and satisfaction of employees is not only a humane approach but also a strategic one for leaders who are looking to plant their flag and make a significant difference in their organization.

People First Leadership is not a fad, it's a movement. And, it's what our evolving workforce is demanding. I want you to win in this leadership game and I know that when you help your people win first, you will be the ultimate victor.

About Jen Buck

Jen Buck is an award-winning Keynote Speaker who has been speaking professionally around the world for 25 years. She's spoken at over 10,000 events, in front of audiences up to 25,000 attendees, impacting over a million people throughout her tenure as a Speaker. Ms. Buck began the first decade of her career in a startup helping to launch a billion-dollar, global and award-winning brand as an employee development Trainer. She understands what it takes to thrive in high-intensity and ever-evolving environments and uses a fast-pace, quick wit, and loads of energy to educate and inspire her audiences. Jen is also a Chief Operating Officer, two-time bestselling author with seven books, a nonprofit founder, former Chief of Staff for three US Congressional campaigns, and currently leading 30,000 people. Jen Buck isn't just talking about leadership from stages, she's doing it every day.

https://www.jenbuckspeaks.com

Instagram: *https://www.instagram.com/jenbuckspeaks*

Facebook: *https://www.facebook.com/JenBuckSpeaks*

LinkedIn: *www.linkedin.com/in/jenbuckspeaks*

TikTok *https://www.tiktok.com/@jenbuckspeaks?t=8hkkE3g666l&_r=1*

YouTube: *https://youtube.com/c/JenBuckSpeaks*

Hospitality: Leadership Lessons From Restaurants

Madeleine Geach

The Smile That Fades Too Quickly

I met Arick when I first started working in restaurants. He was a dedicated, caring manager. And a lot of fun to work with. He taught me a lesson in hospitality, and why it matters to put people who work for you first, in one concise image.

You are in a beautiful restaurant anticipating a wonderful evening ahead. Your waiter comes to your table and welcomes you. She is warm, engaging, recommending dishes and seeming to genuinely care. As she finishes up taking your order, she beams a smile. She turns to take the ticket to the kitchen and you catch her profile. The smile fades. Quickly. Because it was not real. She can't be genuinely happy with you, because she is not happy at work.

Your customers and clients will feel when they are being looked after by someone who is genuinely happy at work. It will affect every part of their experience. Putting your people first pays off. Treat your employees like you treat your guests; happy staff equals happy customers. And the rest will fall into place.

The Warmest Welcome

Working in restaurants I've learnt the importance of beginnings and endings. Customers (or guests, as we call them) remember best the first and last things that happen. It doesn't matter how good the meal is - if you don't get a warm greeting at the reservations desk as you come in, or a proper goodbye as you leave the building, your memories of the evening will be dampened. Waiters are taught the 60 second rule. In the first minute of being at the table guests should be visited and given some water. The message: don't leave people unattended to at the start of an experience.

Treating your employees like you would a customer means knowing that first impressions count. From the interview process to their first day, week and month with you, a warm welcome builds a strong imprint. I've seen people join companies and been metaphorically left unattended to.

When I work with businesses, I ask them to look at every touchpoint of an employee's first contacts with them and make small tweaks to ensure they are shown warmth and care. This may include getting back to people promptly after interviews, a welcome card and gift, making the onboarding process smooth, planning their first day so they are not left alone, introducing them to people fully, and designing an inspiring induction.

Questions: What first impression do you want to give? How do you ensure new people are warmly welcomed onto your team?

Come As You Are

As the adage goes, people will forget what you did and said but never how you made them feel. We know the most successful businesses make people feel a certain way. Tapping into feelings is how the best marketing succeeds. It's how Nike's 'Just Do It' made us feel motivated, or L'Oréal's 'You're Worth It' boosted our self-esteem. Tapping into how you want your employees to feel is key to the heart-led leadership approach.

'Come as you are' is how I wanted both guests and employees to feel in some of the best restaurants I've helped shape. For guests this means a sense of everyone being welcome. Whether you are a regular or a one-off visitor. Having a budget prix-fixe menu or the full à la carte. Dressed up or down. Dining alone or in a group. All are welcome and made to feel welcome.

For employees coming as you are means being able to be yourself at work and all being welcome. Creating this feeling in people taps into two powerful human instincts – our need to be authentic and to belong. One way this happens in restaurants is around handling of customer complaints.

If you've ever made a complaint in a restaurant and the waiter goes to get their manager this is probably because the waiter is not given autonomy to decide how to deal with the complaint themselves. It's shockingly common. Both the waiter and a disgruntled customer are much happier when the waiter is trained in complaint handling, trusted with the budget (they may want to give a free dish) and allowed to find a solution themselves.

Here's a few ideas of how I have created this feeling of autonomy and belonging in workplaces:

- Avoiding - wherever possible - unnecessary rules, using guidelines and principles instead
- Avoiding uniforms and strict dress codes – letting people express themselves through their fashion choices
- Having robust DEI policies, training, and procedures so all genders, sexualities, races, neurotypes, ages, stages of life, abilities, nationalities are welcome
- Giving the what and not the how: setting goals but letting people work out their own way to get there

- Training a coaching style in your managers so there is less directing and more choice

Questions: How do you want people to feel at work? What can you do to make them feel that way?

Telling The Truth

Building trust with your customers involves delivering – even overdelivering - on your promises. Guests want to be surprised and delighted, not overpromised and undelivered to. If things go wrong (and they do most nights in restaurants!) they want mistakes to be acknowledged and things to be resolved quickly.

The same is true for employees. This begins at the start of their employee journey, with what you promise in the job ad and interview and whether you honour your words. It continues with how you communicate day to day as a leader of the business. When things go silent people fill in the gaps with their own stories, often unpleasant ones. And people like to be kept in the loop about the big picture such as the plans for the year ahead. It makes them feel part of things. Being as transparent as possible, and over-communicating rather than under-communicating, are both key.

Here's one example of telling the truth from my work: making promises to new employees.

Make a promise to employees of what you will deliver, print this in black and white (maybe in your staff manual) and say it at inductions. And then meticulously hold yourselves to account on this. One of the five things we promised all new starters at Hawksmoor was a place they'd feel proud to work. We did this by committing to ethical sourcing, sustainability and charity initiatives and giving a 50% discount so they could 'show off' their workplace to friends and family.

One more example was having a structure for transparent sharing of the big picture from the founders of the company. This included an annual roadshow of visits to each restaurant, to present the plan for the year ahead to every member of staff at every level, and monthly video updates, with live ask the leader segments. Depending on the scale of your business the medium will change. The important principle is for leaders to communicate regularly, probably more often than they think needed, and to be as open and transparent as possible.

Questions: What promises could you make to your people? How can you connect them to the big picture?

Personal Growth

From everything I have experienced running coaching and training programs in the hospitality industry, the magic happens when work becomes a place that you not only learn a job and develop a career but also grow as a person.

You may have heard of Maslow's Hierarchy of Needs.

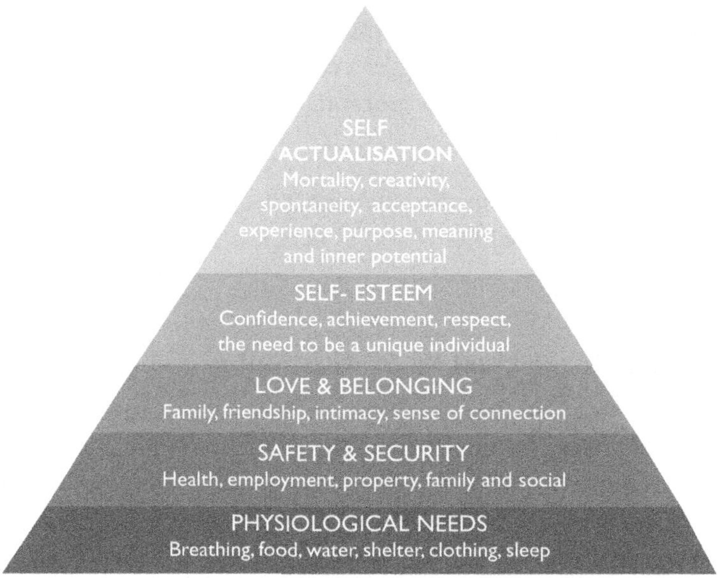

Human beings have five levels of need from 1) physiological (e.g., food and water), 2) security (e.g., contracts) to 3) belonging (e.g., being made to feel welcome at work) to 4) self-esteem (e.g., through being given autonomy). The fifth and highest need is for 'self-actualisation'. This involves fulfilling your potential and personal growth.

Giving your people soft skills training is THE tangible way to achieve this. Soft skills—also known as 'people skills' or 'interpersonal skills'— cover things like resilience, communication, building trust, emotional intelligence, handling change. By their nature training in soft skills helps people manage work. And be good managers for your teams.

I've also frequently been told by managers that soft skills programmes have helped them not just in work but in handling a bumpy patch in their romantic relationship, dealing with a bereavement, improved their parenting, helped them manage their stress so they don't take it home. Maybe you have experienced this yourself? I know I did.

And as an employee this experience is gold. If you can come to work and learn things that impact the quality of your wider life, work begins to fulfil a bigger role – one of allowing you to grow as a person, fulfil your potential and meet your need for self-actualisation.

Question: How can working for you impact people's personal – not just professional - growth?

A Final Word: Hospitality

The hospitality industry inspires me every day. I love that the meaning of hospitality comes from the Latin word *hospes* meaning visitor or guest. It's an industry driven by a desire to take care of people, to welcome them in a warm, friendly, generous way. Restaurants are not just about feeding people.

They are about making them feel good. It's something that is both simple and skilful to do. An art from which we can learn how to treat clients in wider industries. And most importantly here the people who take care of them for us.

The more we treat our employees, too, as our most important guests, the better.

About Madeleine Geach

Madeleine Geach of The Good Life is a culture obsessed Leadership Coach. Working with celebrated chefs, top restaurateurs, and leaders of London's most acclaimed restaurants she helps them to create some of the best places to work - as well as eat – in the country. In recent years she has twice been named one of the Most Influential Women in Hospitality alongside greats like Angela Hartnett and Skye Gyngell (by CODE).

Madeleine was previously Head of Culture at Hawksmoor – shaping the People Team of this widely respected, 1000 person strong restaurant group, voted one of the top places to work in the UK's prestigious Best Companies list every year for over a decade. Hawksmoor is the only restaurant group in the UK to have achieved this. And it did so by putting its people first.

www.thegoodlifecoaching.net

Instagram *@thegoodlifecoaching*

Linked In *Madeleine Geach*

Leading With Kindness

Kylie Denton

I jumped at the chance to be a part of this book because it resonates deeply with my current project on leading with kindness and who wouldn't agree that in today's world the need for kindness is undeniable. My chapter will delve into various aspects, including the scientific underpinnings of kindness, the defining traits of kind leaders, the detrimental effects of unkind leadership, strategies for overcoming obstacles, navigating leadership with kindness amidst pressure, and the evolving landscape of kindness in leadership. However, it's essential to acknowledge that my insights merely scratch the surface of this vast domain.

Every year I am so fortunate to work with over 300 leaders, and when I ask them to share with me leadership qualities, they generally give me words that describe a stereotypical leader. Words like strength, courage, passionate, inspiring, charismatic, trusted, empowering, resilient or people focused, or even strong comes to mind but I think one quality that is not typically high on the list, and yet is absolutely critical for success, is kindness.

Many people think of kindness as a sign of weakness however to me it is a sign of courage and integrity.

I think it's important to point out that when I am referring to kindness, I'm not referring to being nice or a pushover. You can still make those tough decisions and have those tough conversations. It is about making sure that the things you are doing are with kindness in mind. It's about striking a balance between being firm and fair whilst also being kind and supportive.

Karen Ross, an author, defines Kindness as "An action (or set of actions), connecting a person's internal feelings of empathy and compassion to others that is undertaken with purpose of generating a positive effect and outcome for another."

The dictionary defines *kindness* as the quality of being friendly, generous, and considerate.

Kindness as a leader can be giving feedback that people do not want to hear but need to hear.

A friend, colleague, and author, Chris Smoje, once said to me that sometimes being kind to someone is telling them the truth.

It could be dismissing an employee. A few years back I had to dismiss a staff member. I remember going for a walk along this lovely boardwalk near my home, to think about this current situation and whether or not we keep him or we move him on.

As a leader, I recognised the need for kindness while addressing his misfit for the role. The team was affected too, and the culture started suffering. Letting him go was tough but necessary for the team, the business, and him. It allowed him to find a better-suited role. Overall, my actions prioritised kindness for everyone involved.

During the pandemic, Jacinda Ardern, the Prime Minister of New Zealand, addressed criticism suggesting that her empathy made her seem weak because she wasn't perceived as aggressive or assertive. She firmly rejected this notion, asserting that compassion and strength are not mutually exclusive.

Kindness in the workplace is crucial for every business, the benefits are clear, enhanced morale, productivity, and financial performance to name just a few. A simple act of kindness, like a compliment, can significantly brighten someone's day and foster positivity.

Platforms like YouTube showcase numerous instances of kindness, evoking emotional responses. Organisations like The Random Acts of Kindness Foundation advocate for kindness in various settings, including schools and workplaces, underscoring its significance. The COVID-19 pandemic highlighted humanity's kindness, demonstrating its potential to unite communities during crises. Renowned leaders, including Gandhi and Martin Luther King Jr, exemplify how kindness can drive transformative change globally. Simon Sinek emphasises that leaders who genuinely care about their teams are most effective. In one of my books, I underscore the importance of human-centric leadership, advocating for kindness as a core element.

Ultimately, kindness is universally beneficial and should be ingrained in organisational culture.

Let's delve into just some of the fundamental ways in which kindness shapes effective leadership in organisations.

1. Kindness complements leadership traits, fostering connections and collaboration.

2. Kind leaders inspire loyalty and motivation, fostering a positive environment.

3. Kindness creates harmony, boosting morale and productivity.

4. Leaders personally benefit, experiencing improved well-being.

5. Kindness fosters trust, enhancing relationships with teams and clients.

6. Prioritising kindness boosts retention rates in organisations.
7. Kindness strengthens brand reputation and unlocks opportunities.
8. Teams under kind leaders show greater collaboration and innovation.
9. Kindness enhances productivity by supporting a happy workforce.
10. Leading with kindness yields benefits for teams, organisations, and customers.

The role of kindness in leadership cannot be emphasized enough, it not only complements traditional leadership but serves as a catalyst for the future of leadership.

The Science Of Kindness:

Research confirms the psychological and emotional benefits of kindness. Studies by Emmons & McCullough (2003) reveal that gratitude leads to greater happiness and well-being. Positive emotions from acts of kindness, as found by Kok et al. (2013), enhance physical health by increasing vagal nerve activity tone (more simply put, your body's ability to relax and recover efficiently). Tugade, Fredrickson & Barrett (2004) discovered that kindness fosters psychological resilience and aids in stress management. Grant, Courtier & Raines (2015) used fMRI to show brain activation in reward-related regions during acts of kindness. Such studies indicate the positive impact of kindness on mental and emotional well-being.

Embracing kindness in leadership reaps numerous benefits, and believe me, this list only scratches the surface.

- Increased happiness due to endorphin release.
- Reduced stress and anxiety by promoting positive emotions.
- Improved mood through compassionate actions.
- Enhanced relationships, fostering community and social connections.
- Better physical health, including reduced inflammation and improved immunity.

Makes total sense to me that prioritising kindness leads to personal, relational, and societal benefits, making it a compelling approach in leadership.

On the other hand, let's now consider the impact in organisations when we lead without kindness.

Leadership without kindness results in numerous negative consequences. Unkind behaviour creates a toxic work environment, impacting morale, performance, and decreased retention. Unsupportive leaders breed resentment and distrust among team members, hindering communication and collaboration.

Organisations with unkind leaders suffer reputational damage, struggling to attract and retain talent. It's imperative for leaders to cultivate kindness to foster a positive, productive, and enjoyable workplace environment.

Qualities Of Kindness In Leadership

Kind leaders embody numerous qualities that cultivate a culture of kindness. Due to space constraints, I'll highlight some very important qualities that I see in kind leaders.

1. **Kindness to Self & Others:** Establishing boundaries and self-care enables leaders to extend kindness to others, fostering strong relationships.

2. **Leading by Example:** Modelling kindness inspires others to follow suit, emphasising the importance of actions aligning with values.

3. **Offering Praise and Recognition:** Recognising achievements motivates employees, leading to improved performance, retention, and a positive work culture.

4. **Helping vs Blaming:** Shifting from blame to support encourages learning from mistakes, promoting growth and development within the team.

5. **Calling out Bad Behaviour:** As leaders, it's vital to address bad behaviour promptly without turning a blind eye.

6. **Curiosity vs Defensiveness:** Leading with kindness means being curious rather than defensive. This approach builds stronger relationships and creates a positive workplace culture.

7. **Clarity:** Kind leaders communicate goals clearly, reducing misunderstandings and conflict while improving teamwork.

8. **Feedback**: Providing regular, constructive feedback is a hallmark of kind leadership.

9. **Gratitude:** Kind leaders express gratitude for their team members' contributions, fostering pride, motivation, and positive energy within the organisation.

I really struggled to just stop here but hopefully you get the power of these qualities that we see and need in kind leaders.

If the above are the qualities, then let's consider kindness in actions. The actions that kind leaders demonstrate inspire and motivate others toward goals:

1. They give undivided attention, showing genuine interest during interactions.
2. They take time to understand individuals, their backgrounds, interests, and preferences.
3. They ask about well-being and listen attentively with empathy.
4. They seek opportunities to assist others.
5. They offer genuine compliments on work, fostering positivity.
6. They assume positive intentions, avoiding blame and promoting understanding.
7. They prioritise letting others speak first, encouraging participation and inclusivity.

As a leader, where do you need to put more focus on, in your actions?

Overcoming Barriers To Kindness

In my work with leaders across various industries, especially healthcare, I emphasise the importance of recognising triggers that may lead to unkind behaviour. Triggers activate our fight or flight response, influencing how we treat our team and those around us.

Identifying triggers, whether from work stress or personal issues, enhances self-awareness and response management.

Leaders should introspect on what irks them, whether it's rudeness, incomplete tasks, workload, or personal stressors. Recognising triggers allows for more mindful reactions. Triggers vary among individuals, so understanding one's unique triggers is crucial for effective leadership.

When we understand our triggers, we can start to consider how we might approach it in a kind way?

- What are some of the things that you do when something or someone triggers you?
- How are you reacting in the moment?
- How are you keeping your calm so that you do not be unkind?
- What do you do?
- What do you need to do differently?

One thing we know about leadership is we need leaders that are consistent. People don't want leaders that are inconsistent with their behaviour, one day happy, the next cranky and unkind.

> *"Kindness is a balance - you are not going to be rainbows and sunshine every day - but there must be consistency."*

Leading With Kindness Under Pressure

Leading with kindness under pressure is challenging due to the demands of high-stress environments. However, it's vital for fostering strong, trusted teams. While it's commonly believed that character emerges under pressure, this notion isn't always precise. Research indicates that behaviours exhibited during stressful situations may not consistently align with one's true character. Instead, they are often influenced by a multitude of factors, including personal beliefs and past experiences.

Here are some key strategies for leading with kindness under pressure:

- **Practice Empathy:** Understand team members' feelings and experiences.
- **Communication:** Be transparent about challenges and setbacks.
- **Show Appreciation:** Recognise efforts and express gratitude.
- **Be Compassionate:** Understand others' perspectives and practice self-compassion.
- **Provide Support:** Ensure resources and support are available for success.
- **Foster Collaboration:** Encourage teamwork and mutual support.
- **Set Clear Expectations:** Define roles and goals clearly.
- **Practice Self-care:** Prioritise mental and emotional well-being.
- **Stay Positive:** Maintain optimism and spread positivity.
- **Express Thanks:** Acknowledge and appreciate team members' efforts.
- **Grow Resilience:** Learn from challenges and inspire optimism in others.
- **Look for the Good:** Recognise strengths in team members.
- **Use Humour:** Lighten the mood to reduce stress and improve camaraderie.
- **Practice Humility:** Learn from mistakes and seek input from others.

The Kindness Culture

In fostering a cultural shift, personal initiative is paramount. We must refrain from exacerbating negativity and instead focus on personal growth. Despite a company's overarching culture, teams can cultivate their own ethos. Leaders play a pivotal role in championing kindness amid adversity, facilitating supportive environments. Encouraging kindness entails several actions:

1. **Courageous Intervention:** Brené Brown advocates courage over comfort in addressing unkindness.
2. **Supportive Presence**: Offer reassurance and solidarity to those experiencing unkindness. Simply being there and saying, "I've got you," can make a significant difference.
3. **Fostering Belonging:** Make individuals feel valued and understood, and included.
4. **Brand of Kindness:** Consider the keywords you want associated with your kindness. Reflect on what you want people to say about you when you're not in the room. This exercise aids in living and promoting a personal brand of kindness.

Promoting kindness is an ongoing journey of personal development and organisational transformation. By embodying kindness, we leave a legacy of compassion and positivity now and into the future.

The Future Of Kindness In Leadership

The landscape of leadership has transformed significantly since my entry into the workforce in 1989. Initially characterised by a hierarchical "command and control" structure, where leaders wielded unilateral decision-making power, this era instilled a top-down approach and one I hated. My own experience vividly recalls one instance of public reprimand, fuelling my resolve to lead with empathy and respect in the future.

In recent years, a paradigm shift has occurred, emphasising collaboration and empowerment. This transition arises from various factors, including shifts in business dynamics and a growing emphasis on employee engagement. Today, I witness leaders embracing a collaborative style, where that collective input fosters stronger outcomes. Collaboration, trust, and unity emerge as essential ingredients for success.

As leadership evolves, the concept of leading with kindness will gain prominence. Research underscores the pivotal role of leaders in employee retention and satisfaction.

Poor relationships with managers often drive employees to seek alternative employment opportunities. Consequently, leaders bear the responsibility of fostering positive work environments, characterised by empathy and support, to retain top talent and ensure organisational success.

This chapter merely scratches the surface of the immense power inherent in leading with kindness. Be on the lookout for my upcoming book, where I delve deeply into the profound impact of kindness in leadership. As a final thought, let me highlight the truly transformative nature of kindness.

1. **Embodying Excellence:** Kind leaders epitomise virtues like empathy, compassion, and authenticity, fostering an atmosphere of trust and collaboration within their teams.
2. **Inspiring Action:** Their actions, of understanding and support, serve as a beacon, igniting inspiration and motivating others to follow their example.
3. **Overcoming Adversity:** Even in the face of adversity, they confront obstacles with kindness, particularly in high-pressure situations.

4. **Fostering Success:** By fostering a culture of kindness within organisations, they not only enhance well-being but also inspire and propel success to unprecedented levels.

In shaping the future of leadership, prioritising kindness emerges as a cornerstone. By creating environments where empathy and compassion flourish, we pave the way for enduring greatness.

I hope these insights have allowed you to reflect on where you excel in kindness and a roadmap for you to continue your growth in kindness whilst also considering how you can create a culture of kindness in your organisation.

About Kylie Denton

Kylie Denton is a highly experienced leadership consultant, professionally certified coach, a bestselling author, and speaker specialising in leadership and sales. With over 30 years' experience in leadership and formal qualifications in psychology, she has a proven track record in building confident leaders and successful teams. Kylie works with established companies to improve the productivity and performance of leaders and their teams. Kylie delivers high-energy keynote presentations and workshops throughout North America, Europe and Australasia that inspire her audience to become better in a world that desperately needs strong leadership.

Kylie has inspired people throughout the Financial Services, Health, Education, Government Industries and has worked across large and small organisations in both public and private sectors including blue chip companies like Suncorp, NAB, QSuper, Blue Care, Griffith University, RACQ and Brighter Super.

Kylie@performanceadvisorygroup.com.au

https://performanceadvisorygroup.com.au

Facebook *https://www.facebook.com/softskillsau*

Facebook Community *https://www.facebook.com/groups/performanceadvisorygroupau/*

Instagram *https://www.instagram.com/performanceadvisorygroup*

LinkedIn *https://www.linkedin.com/in/kyliedenton5*

LinkedIn Company page: *https://bit.ly/49JSlgo*

YouTube: *https://bit.ly/3UVkFlx*

Leading High-Performing Heart-Led Teams

Andrew Priestley

In 2030, Millennials will outnumber Boomers. Right now they want to be lead differently. Right now, we are seeing one of the biggest trends on the planet – top talent leaving top companies because of poor leadership.

And in a few, very fast years, they *will* lead differently.

A key study is Google's Aristotle Project, which is a great resource and philosophical starting point if you are considering heart-led, high performing teams.

For those unfamiliar, the Aristotle Project was a ground breaking initiative aimed at understanding what makes a team truly effective. The study emphasises that success isn't solely about having the best and brightest individuals, but rather, it hinges on how team members interact and collaborate.

This chapter explores how you can implement key insights from these studies into your people to foster heart-led innovation, creativity and ultimately success in your business.

The Aristotle Project identified five key insights when it comes to fostering highly effective teams:

1. Psychological Safety: Creating A Safe Space For Ideas And Nurturing Creative-Expression

The study identified *psychological safety* as the bedrock of effective teams. It means I can trust you. This means team members *feel* comfortable taking risks, sharing ideas, and expressing themselves without fear of judgment. Cultivating an environment where everyone's voice is heard - and valued - can spark creativity, innovation and problem-solving.

Encourage open communication, actively listen to diverse perspectives, and celebrate failure as a learning opportunity. By doing so, you lay the foundation for a team that thrives on creativity and continuous improvement.

This is not possible unless and until you *genuinely* place people at the heart of your business.

2. Dependability: Trusting Each Other's Commitments

The study clearly identified that *dependability* is crucial. It means I can rely on you. Each team member must trust that their colleagues – and leaders – will deliver on their commitments. Google found that reliable teams were more likely to take risks, if they knew they genuinely had a safety net of support.

Implementing this in your teams involves setting clear expectations, ensuring accountability, and fostering a culture where trust is not just an expectation but a core value.

When trust is established, team members can focus on their unique strengths, knowing they can rely on others to complement their skills.

In a smaller team, trust and dependability become even more critical. Each member plays a significant role, and trusting that everyone will contribute their expertise is key. Establish clear lines of communication, set realistic expectations, and foster a culture where each team member's contribution is valued. This creates a dependable foundation upon which our small team can confidently pursue innovative or ambitious projects.

3. Structure And Clarity: Defining Roles And Goals

The study emphasises the importance of providing clear goals and well-defined roles within a team. It means I know what I am doing and what I am required to do.

You can start by clarifying and setting clear objectives, outlining individual responsibilities, and ensuring that everyone understands their contribution to the overarching goals. This is a great argument for also implementing Objectives and Key Results (OKRs). Clarity not only enhances efficiency but also empowers team members to leverage their strengths in pursuit of shared objectives.

Studies show that the team now want to be a part of deciding what that all looks like. That is a people-first imperative if you are genuine about putting people first.

Specialisation is often a strength. You might create specific roles within your small team to capitalise on individual strengths and skills. Obviously, these need to align with the vision and mission of the enterprise so carefully explore responsibilities, ensuring that each member understands their unique contribution to your shared beauty goals. This structured approach enhances efficiency and allows for a seamless collaboration especially in a close-knit team.

4. Meaning: Connecting To A Greater Purpose

Studies demonstrate that successful teams are driven by a shared sense of purpose. What this means is what I do matters; and it matters – to me personally – what I am doing. Teams with a strong sense of meaning outperform those who lack that certainty about the impact of their daily work. In an entrepreneurial context, aligning your team with a shared vision and mission can fuel motivation and resilience.

Regularly communicate the broader purpose of your venture, emphasizing the impact it can have on customers, communities, or industries. When team members feel connected to a higher purpose, they are more likely to invest their energy and creativity in overcoming challenges.

Understand that individuals are more motivated by their own meaningful intrinsic motivations that meaningless extrinsic incentives.

Studies show that Millennials want to make personally meaningful and relevant contributions.

5. Impact: It Matters And Counts

The study emphasised that not only do we draw personal meaning and purpose from our roles, but that what we are doing positively impacts our customers, if not the planet. This means what I do matters to others. It counts. It makes a difference. Leading from the heart takes is a significant driver of impact.

Clearly, what drives the success of the above principles is an authentic heart-led, people-first approach that sits at the core of your values. You cannot pay these lip service because your top A-game talent will vote with their feet! A very real consequence of ignoring these principles is a team of B players!

So, What Happens When Leaders Fail To Implement The Principles Outlined Above?

Here are ten potential issues that can occur:

1. **Lack of Psychological Safety:** Without a focus on creating a psychologically safe environment, team members will increasingly feel hesitant to express their ideas, leading to a stifling of creativity and innovation. Or worse they leave and go to where they *do* feel safe! And to where they *feel* valued.

2. **Poor Team Collaboration:** Failure to emphasise the importance of dependability and trust - *and trust IS the glue* – can easily result in poor collaboration and breakdowns in communication, hindering the team's ability to work together effectively... and inhibit the results and impacts you want to achieve.

3. **Role Ambiguity:** If leaders do not provide clarity on roles and responsibilities, team members easily experience confusion and frustration, leading to inefficiency and potential conflicts.

4. **Absent Structure:** The absence of a clear structure within the team can lead to chaos, as members may struggle to understand how their contributions fit into the larger picture, affecting overall productivity. Understand poor productivity is an expensive yet avoidable indulgence.

5. **Lack of Motivation and Meaning:** Neglecting to connect the team's work to a broader purpose increasingly now results in decreased motivation and engagement, impacting the quality and enthusiasm with which tasks are approached.

6. **Increased Turnover/Attrition of Top Talent:** When team members do not feel psychologically safe or lack trust in their colleagues, job satisfaction may decline, increasing the likelihood they will vote with their feet... and CVs. Top talent attrition is now THE most expensive recruitment issue on the planet.

7. **Ineffective Problem Solving:** Without a foundation of psychological safety and openness, teams struggle to address and resolve challenges, leading to persistent issues that can hinder progress. Imagine a business that does not solve problems that benefit all stakeholders. Not a nice picture, right?

8. **Decreased Innovation:** Failure to foster an environment where diverse perspectives are valued can definitely limit the team's ability to generate innovative ideas and find creative solutions to problems. Understand, innovation drives efficiencies... which drive capacity... which drive revenues... and profit... and cashflow. You need to contemplate the knock-on effect – commercially – of decreased innovation.

9. **Resistance to Change:** Teams that do not feel secure resist changes in processes or strategies, hindering the organisation's ability to adapt to evolving market demands or industry trends. (They can also express their insecurity in subtle and passive-aggressive ways!)

10. **Diminished Team Morale:** The cumulative effect of the above issues can result in lower team morale... creating a negative work atmosphere... that impacts productivity, employee satisfaction, and overall organisational success. A business that fails on its remit, vision and mission risks becoming an also-ran or worse, reputation damage.

In essence, neglecting the principles identified in the Aristotle Project can lead to a cascade of challenges that impede your team's ability to reach its full potential and contribute to the organisation's success.

New To All This?

Finally, if you are brand new to the heart-led philosophy, here's what you might focus on during your first 12 months. Here are some key unique challenges, considerations and potential obstacles:

1. **Resource Constraints:** Small businesses often operate with limited resources, including time, personnel, and budget. Implementing these principles may require investments in training, tools, and cultural shifts, which can strain the available resources.

2. **Limited Team Size:** Straight up, the principles were initially designed for larger teams. Adapting them to smaller teams can be challenging, as the dynamics and challenges in smaller groups differ significantly.

3. **Establishing Psychological Safety:** Creating an environment of psychological safety can be challenging in a small team where personal relationships may be more pronounced. Team members may be hesitant to voice concerns or share ideas if they fear it might impact their relationships. This highlights the key challenge of being that heart-lead leader!

4. **Defining Clear Roles:** In smaller teams, individuals often wear multiple hats, and role definitions may not be as clear-cut. Defining and communicating roles while maintaining flexibility can be a delicate balance.

5. **Limited Diversity:** Small teams may lack the diversity seen in larger organisations, both in terms of skills and perspectives which can impact the richness of discussions and problem-solving.

6. **Scaling Solutions:** This chapter emphasises a focus on effective management practices, that may require adjustments for smaller teams. Scaling down processes and solutions while maintaining effectiveness can be challenging.

7. **Time Management:** Small business owners and team members often wear multiple hats and have busy schedules. Carving out time for training, team-building activities may be challenging.

8. **Resistance to Change:** Small businesses may have established routines and practices that are deeply ingrained. Introducing new principles may face resistance, especially if they are perceived as disrupting the existing workflow.

9. **Balancing Short-Term Goals and Long-Term Vision:** In the early stages of a small business, there is often a focus on immediate tasks and survival. Balancing the implementation of long-term principles with the urgency of short-term demands can be a significant challenge.

10. **Measuring Success:** Establishing metrics for success and measuring the impact of these principles in a small business context may be challenging. Clear benchmarks need to be set to evaluate the effectiveness of the implementation.

To address these challenges, a tailored approach that considers the unique characteristics of the small business, along with ongoing support and guidance, will be crucial. Regular assessments, feedback loops, and adjustments will help ensure a successful integration of the above principles in the first 12 months and beyond.

In conclusion, it's worthwhile embracing the principles of psychological safety, dependability, structure, meaning and impact from Google's Aristotle Project, especially with a smaller close-knit team.

The obvious conclusion is none of this is possible unless and until you explore how to consciously implement a heart-led, people first leadership approach.

It *can* be done. *This book shows you how!*

About Andrew Priestley

Andrew Priestley is an award-winning business leadership coach, ranked in the Top 100 UK Mentors, an in-demand keynote speaker, and multi-bestselling author qualified in industrial and organisational psychology.

He created the Business Leadership Profile which is used by companies worldwide to benchmark the leadership skills, strengths and weaknesses of their key managers executives; and design bespoke, high impact leadership coaching programs.

www.andrewpriestley.com

andrew@andrewpriestley.com

https://andrewpriestley.com/lets-chat/

https://www.linkedin.com/in/andrewpriestley/

Every Act Of Business Can Be An Act Of Love

Amanda Winwood

You may be wondering what I mean by that. It's a good question and you will not be the first person to question this. Why do I believe that leading from the heart and being kind is an absolute strength for any business? Well here goes and I hope that you make take some thoughts away that help you.

First of all, I do know the absolute validity and essential requirement to be profitable within a business. Note the word profit not turnover! However, how you do this and your "why" is also essential in terms of what and how you run your business – whatever that is. My belief is that if what you do in life is not led from the heart and doesn't make you want to leap out of bed in the morning with purpose and drive, don't do it. Life is too short.

Another question that is fundamental to me is: Do you know what your brand or business does to make a difference (profits) people's lives along the way?

Some people may still think that huge monetary profits are the core of greatness. However, if I asked you "who do you think is a great leader?" I am not sure your reply would be based on monetary wealth alone. I don't believe that there a single business owner on the planet who would not welcome a healthy bank balance and the ability to pay any suppliers with ease. It is what many of us dream of at times! But do you sleep well at night, knowing that you have done your best, by you and your team? how easy are your relationships with customers? Do you love and respect them? Do they love and respect you? This really matters.

I have done many things in my life – from being the youngest licensee in Liverpool back in 1983, to being Head of Tourism on Tower Bridge in the 1990's. I have run hotels and organised events for up to 1,000 people. There is one common thread that created success in every single business – the quality of the relationships with the team that I worked with and the people that were my customers. I have also made many mistakes along the way and often ignored the good counsel of others, but that is simply life and making mistakes are a great way of learning. Just don't repeat them!

My view is that there are some simple fundamentals that every human being needs, to feel good about what they do and who they are. We are all worthy of love and to be loved. In spite of our imperfections, we are all doing our best in life. None of us are perfect and that's where I believe the following words are vital in every relationship whether it is work or business:

- Love
- Honesty
- Truth
- Respect

Without these, we have nothing. What does this mean in practice in business? Well for us, we have ended relationships with customers who have been rude to our team, who haven't paid on time and who are just simply what I would term a "mood hoover". I have another acronym for people like this, but I won't share otherwise this may never make it to being published!

I will give you an example. We had, what should have been, an amazing contract with a really prestigious five-star hotel. The whole team were thrilled, and we thought it would be great for the business. But we made a mistake. The contract put a huge pressure on our lovely team and us too. There were constant invalid complaints via phone and email to us and our team, changes to volumes and our cash flow and actual profit were hammered!

We found that the behaviours we encountered were NOT heart-led behaviour or respectful, so we talked with the team, reviewed everything, apologised for the stress it had caused them and then just called it a day. It was a huge relief! So... be brave, take a deep breath and make decisions with your heart and gut, with a good dollop of intelligence thrown in. Finish any business relationship that doesn't serve you or your team well. I have a wonderful friend who calls this "the Sacred NO".

What is your why?

Your "why" is the essence of who you are and why you do what you do. It comes from way down deep inside you. Often, we will try and repress this feeling or change it to fit around what we believe we should do or be. It is so important to understand who you are, and what your purpose is. When you run your business or lead your team, take time to check in and validate this. It is simply your authentic you.

It is also essential to ensure that your work does not become all encompassing. Whatever you do in work should reflect who you are but not define you. Family, health, love, respect, compassion, privacy, and security are all essentials for us to grow and flourish. The same goes for anyone we work with, and it is important to remember that their values and view of life may be different to yours. Take time to step back and put yourself in other people's shoes. It will help.

Our "why"/purpose should extend and include those who support us – family, friends, and the team we work with. If your 'fan base' don't have your back and love the very bones of your brand and what you do, you will not lead them to where your vision is. This is the essence of a great business. It all sounds simple on paper but…leading a team and ensuring that they feel secure, confident and motivated takes time, energy, and effort. And you definitely won't get things right all the time so don't beat yourself up when it goes Pete Tong!

My belief (and learning) is that heart-led leadership is a fine balance. It is about you making sure that you look after your team and ensuring that they feel that they have clarity on their tole within the business and are respected. However, clear, and open communication is a two-way process. It is an essential part of what needs to happen to make sure that everyone understands that they own their attitude and are part of creating a positive vibe. Good energy out = good energy in!

When you are thinking about your team and looking after them, check that you are sticking to your values and thinking about what you need to be well and resilient too. I have often had to put on what I terms as the 'pants of power' to deal with difficult situations. They are imaginary and are like Wonder Woman's, but I have been known to wear a pair on stage once or twice!

Honest conversations based on a good set of values really help. Ours are:

- Honesty
- Respect
- Ethical
- Support
- Innovation
- Passion

Make sure that you have your values in place, right at the start, and ensure that they are part of the interview process and every conversation. This will enable you to have really clear and open conversations which may not always be easy but if they always centre on your values, you will be OK. More than OK. You will be AWESOME! If people have a different set of values or theirs come from a different place, they may not be the right people to work with. Let them go and wish them well.

If your communication always comes from a place of compassion, care and concern it will work in letting people know that you care. Say you are sorry when you get it wrong. This opens up the ability for people to be open and make mistakes, which is essential because we learn from mistakes. It's also important that people feel secure enough to push boundaries and make those mistakes. Before you have a conversation, take time to catch the breath and consider what other people may be feeling.

It will serve you well.

It is a joy and also tough running any business. That is the rollercoaster of being free to make decisions but also being accountable for everything you decide – it's a big gig! What I have learned, and this is really important.... is that there is something essential about looking after yourself and your own wellbeing in the midst of everything too. Whilst looking after others emotional wellbeing, think about your own too.

You may find this acronym useful too, shared by a good friend with an epic career in senior finance for a multi-national company. He said "Things will not always go right but Fail equals":

- First
- Attempt
- In
- Learning

When things don't go right, keep a little record of what went well, what didn't and REMEMBER when a similar event crops up what you did well and what you didn't.

My lovely eldest daughter who is a psychology graduate and wise beyond her years, gave me another acronym – HALT. What does that mean? It means NEVER (and I mean NEVER) make any important decision when you are:

- Hungry (for love or nourishment in any form)
- Angry
- Lonely
- Tired

If you have a decision to make and you recognise that you are feeling one or more of these emotions, please, please do not make a decision that affects you, your business, or your team.

Take a little time to catch the breath, be still and perhaps speak to someone you trust and take time to reflect on what they say. Go for a walk, listen to some music, and just feel what you feel, and you will be fine.

And my final thoughts for you are these:

Remember that the plan is not always the path. Our business was inspired by a love of nature and a fundamental belief that there was a way to create a happier and healthier world through organic skincare. It became so much more. I had no idea when started out in 2003 how we many lives we would touch and how fulfilling that would be personally and professionally.

When I found out in 2006 that 98% of people with cancer who went to a spa were being turned away it was a shock. My hugest heart-led achievement has been, working alongside an awesome team, to change this statistic and to enable the spa sector (and now hospices) to warmly welcome people living with cancer for some beautiful wellbeing.

This still makes me leap out of bed in the morning, 21 years on, with a heart full of hope and love. That's how you lead. You don't need to have a great big company to do great things. Just a great team and a big heart and...occasionally "pants of power"! Go change lives and remember it may be much better to be remembered for being "mint" rather than "minted".

About Amanda Winwood

Amanda Winwood, CEO (and Queen of Hugs) Made for Life Organics (B Corp accredited) and Founder of the Made for Life Foundation (Charity 1138846). Amanda has pioneered ethical and sustainable organic skincare that is suitable for sensitive skin and promoted accessible wellness and inclusivity for 21 years. Her belief is that connecting people with the power of plants though organic skincare creates a healthier and happier world. Amanda has over 42 years' senior experience, in hospitality and tourism including launching corporate hospitality onto Tower Bridge.

Amanda, with the Made for Life team have trained over 2000 therapists across the UK to confidently open their doors to people living with cancer and other long term health issues. The education has extended into colleges and hospices with an award winning and fully accredited training course. Amanda was awarded a Lifetime Achievement award by the UKSA in recognition for her work with Cancer Touch Therapy and sits on the Board of the SATCC (Standards Authority for Touch in Cancer Care). A published author, accomplished speaker, therapist, Reiki Master, with Diplomas in Shinrin Yoku, and Mindfulness Amanda was also awarded Freedom of the City of London in 1994.

Above all she is a lover of life.

*@madeforlife_*

@madeforlifeorganics

@madeforlifeorganics

Amanda Winwood/Made for Life Organics

www.madeforlifeorganics.com

Would You Like To Contribute To Leading From The Heart?

Leading From The Heart - relational leadership – is growing and evolving on a daily basis. This book contains fine examples of the innovative thinking that has bought relational leadership to life in a variety of enterprises.

The idea of this book is to allow leaders around the world to share their best-practice stories for the mutual benefit of everyone.

We are actively looking for new contributors for our next edition of Leading From The Heart. If you are a professional in a leadership role and would like to get involved in the next release, then get in touch. All you need is a good story to share that you know will add value to the readership.

If you would like to express your interest please contact Joan Scott at: *joanscottie7@gmail.com*

Printed in Great Britain
by Amazon

39428191R00108